PAINT
WITH THE *Pros*

*G*ather some brushes and acrylic paints, find a comfortable painting spot, and enjoy the opportunity to paint with America's top decorative artists. The talented contributors to this book have turned their love for decorative painting into lifetime careers of teaching others how to paint. Often referred to as "Big Brushes" for their celebrity in the field of decorative painting, they have taught countless numbers of students at seminars and conventions around the world, as well as in books, videos, and television appearances.

In this book each artist shares a lesson focused on a favorite technique or subject. They then take you step-by-step through the painting process to create a beautiful project. Get started with the basics, then move on to special brush and strokework techniques. Experiment with special painting styles, such as trompe l'oeil or Norwegian Rosemaling, and learn to paint some of today's most popular decorative painting subjects—fruit, flowers, landscapes, animals and folk art. Finding the best teacher is never a problem when you Paint with the Pros!

PRODUCED BY KOOLER DESIGN STUDIO, INC

Acknowledgments

Special thanks to the talented artists/teachers who have shared their experise and beautiful projects in this book: Arlene Beck, Sharyn Binam, Debbie Cole, Dorothy Dent, Donna Dewberry, Priscilla Hauser, Jo Sonja Jansen, Andy B. Jones, Phillip C. Myer, Gayle Oram, Heather Redick, Vi Thurmond, and Marsha Weiser. It has been a privilege and a pleasure to work with so many gifted decorative artists. —Judy Swager, Editor

10 9 8 7 6 5 4 3 2 1

Library of Congress Cataloging-in-Publication Data
   Kooler, Donna
   Paint With The Pros
   "A Leisure Arts Publication"

   I S B N :   1 - 5 7 4 8 6 - 3 1 3 - 4

PRODUCED BY
Kooler Design Studio, Inc. • 399 Taylor Blvd., Ste. 104
Pleasant Hill, CA 94523 • kds@koolerdesign.com
Creative Director, Donna Kooler • Editor, Judy Swager
Biography Writer/Proofreader, Kit Schlich • Proofreader, Barbara Kuhn
Production Assistants, Jessica Main, Barbara Hillman, Sandy Orton
Photography, Dianne Woods • Photo Stylist, Basha Kooler Hanner

PUBLISHED BY

Border design by Jo Sonja Jansen

Contents

Getting Started by Sharyn Binam, CDA, CCD, CPD 2

Acrylic Sideload by Sharyn Binam, CDA, CCD, CPD 9
   PROJECT: Seashell Treasures 14

Brush Techniques by Debbie Cole, CDA 21
   PROJECT: Blossom 26

Strokework by Heather Redick, CDA 31
   PROJECT: Strokework Floral 38

Paint and Faux Finishes
   by Phillip C. Myer and Andy B. Jones, CDA 41
   PROJECT: Champagne and Roses 46

One-Stroke Painting by Donna Dewberry 51
   PROJECT: Roses and Violets 56

Norwegian Rosemaling by Gayle Oram, MDA, VGM 61
   PROJECT: Os Tray 64

Trompe L'Oeil by Marsha Weiser, CDA 71
   PROJECT: Salad Fixings 76

Painting Fruit by Priscilla Hauser 81
   PROJECT: Fruit Favorites .84

Painting Flowers by Arlene Beck, MDA 91
   PROJECT: Sweet Pea Jewels 94

Painting Landscapes by Dorothy Dent 101
   PROJECT: Tea House 104

Painting Animals by Vi Thurmond, MDA 111
   PROJECT: Kitten Basket 114

Folk Art Painting by Jo Sonja Jansen, MDA, VGM 119
   PROJECT: Bride's Box 122

Artists/Sources 127

Getting Started

By Sharyn Binam, CDA, CCD, CPD

BEGINNING TO PAINT

Decorative painting techniques offer a wonderful method of learning to paint. Patterns are included for most designs, and techniques are taught in progressive steps with an emphasis on basic skills. With a structured method for mastering the terminology and techniques and then practicing new skills, you'll enjoy unraveling the mysteries of painting.

Always read the instructions for each project before starting to better understand the steps involved, how each is accomplished, what the effect will be, and why. As in learning any other skill, mastering decorative painting techniques requires practice. For best results, practice first on heavy paper or cardboard before painting on your chosen surface. And remember, a mistake can be an opportunity to learn.

ORGANIZING SUPPLIES

Acquire the basic equipment: palette, palette knife, paints, water basin, brushes, transfer supplies and surface preparation supplies (see box below). A little organization can help make the most of your painting time, so start by organizing your painting supplies in a convenient location. If a permanent painting area is not available, a rolling cart can easily move supplies for quick set up and tear down. Keep the most-used items, such as brushes, transfer supplies, water basin, palette, and mediums, on top for easy access.

Keep an organized and tidy work area to minimize accidents while painting. Organize necessities within easy reach. A plastic literature holder, available at office supplies stores, is useful for holding and protecting instructions, photographs, and transfer supplies. It provides the maximum amount of organization in the least amount of space. Empty paint bottles or small plastic containers are handy for holding cotton swabs, pencils, pens, stylus, or other materials at easy reach.

Read the instructions for projects and make a list of needed supplies. Keep specialty supplies, hardware, accessories, instructions, pattern, photographs, and tracings with the project piece. Seal and basecoat several pieces at one time. When dry, store them in plastic bags and you'll be all set for your next painting sessions.

ACRYLIC PAINTS

The projects in this book are painted with acrylic paints which decorative artists appreciate for their great versatility. Acrylics can be used (similar to oils or

BASIC SUPPLIES

- **Paints**
- **Palette, palette knife**
- **Water basin**
- **Brushes**
- **Paper towels**
- **Transfer Supplies:** Tracing paper, permanent marking pen, pencil, ruler, stylus, graphite transfer paper, white chalk paper or *Super Chacopaper*, eraser, painter's tape, ruler, scissors, French curves, circle guides
- **Surface Prep Supplies:** See pages 5– 7 for various surfaces

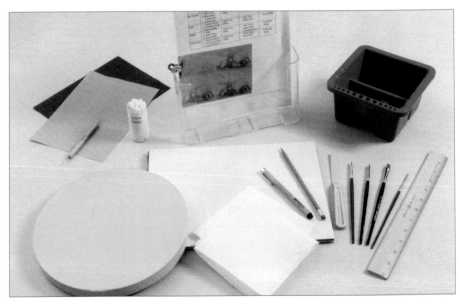

Organizing your painting supplies within easy reach makes painting more enjoyable. A plastic literature holder is useful for holding and protecting instructions, photographs, and transfer supplies.

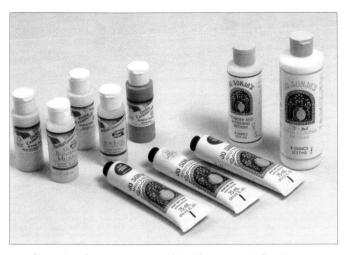

Acrylics paints have great versatility. Shown are Delta Ceramcoat *bottle acrylics and mediums (left) and* Jo Sonja *acrylic gouache and mediums (right).*

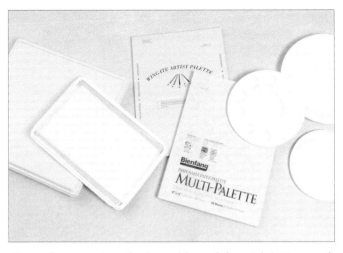

Choose from a variety of palettes: (shown left to right) Masterson's Sta-Wet Palette, deli-paper wet palette, Wingate Palette, waxed palette pad, bubble/divided palette, Styrofoam plate, plastic lid.

watercolor) on canvas, wood, fabric, and paper. All three types of paint are colored with the same pigments, only the vehicle or binding agents differ. Linseed oil or safflower oil holds the pigment in oil paints; gum arabic is the binder for watercolors; and acrylic polymer is the binder for acrylics. Acrylics dry rapidly and are permanent and waterproof when dry. The paint remains somewhat flexible and will expand and contract with surface changes. How lightfast or permanent a color is varies with the pigments used and the quality of the paint. Most acrylic products are non-toxic.

Tube acrylics are thick and creamy. They can be thinned with various mediums including water. Since they are thick, use a palette knife rather than a brush to mix them on the palette. Tube paints are preferred for canvas painting and for palette knife techniques.

Bottle acrylics have the convenience of a large choice of pre-mixed colors with a consistency that does not require thinning except for line work. Several brands are available; each is unique and should be used with the mediums and finishes developed by the manufacturer for maximum compatibility. Store acrylic paints at room temperature to avoid damage

from extreme temperature changes. Shake paint thoroughly to mix the binder and pigment since they separate when stored. Acrylics tend to dry quickly, so place only small amounts of paint out on the palette and refresh frequently. Fresh paint is easiest to control.

Acrylic gouache is similar to watercolor gouache. It has the blending capabilities of oil paint yet is non-toxic. This paint can be reactivated even when dry unless it is sealed. Many traditional strokework techniques are more luminous in acrylic gouache. Like bottled acrylics, gouache has its own complements of extenders and blending mediums. Many painters enjoy using a commercial wet palette with acrylic gouache as it enables them to keep paint mixes workable.

PALETTE

A palette provides a place to lay out paint puddles and also provides a working surface for blending. Place paint puddles along the top edge of the palette and use the remainder for blending. A messy palette has a greater accident potential than a neat palette. Never reach across the palette; keep it on the right side if right-handed and opposite if left-handed.

A Styrofoam plate or plastic lid makes an inexpensive palette for basecoating, some types of strokework, or for mixing glazes and washes. Plastic bubble and divided palettes are useful for mixing colors and mixing mediums with paint.

The traditional palette used by acrylic painters is a waxed palette. The waxed paper sheets are bound into a pad and do not absorb the acrylic paint. Sheets can be thrown away after a painting session. An alternative to the traditional waxed palettes is the *Wingate Palette* which has extra heavy paper that can be washed many times.

Since acrylic paints dry quickly on a waxed palette, many painters prefer to use a wet palette which provides a source of moisture to keep the paint usable for longer periods. A simple wet palette is made with lightly waxed, inexpensive deli paper. I use *Kabnet Wax* brand, purchased in boxes of 1000 sheets at a discount store. Fold the paper in half and insert a folded piece of white paper towel between the folded sheet. Wet the combined deli sheet/towel "palette" and place in a shallow tray or on a waxed palette. The center towel provides moisture and stability. For additional moisture, add a piece of artificial chamois (found in automotive departments) as a liner in the tray. Squeeze out excess water as you smooth out the palette paper and wipe away any water drops. You may wish to purchase a commercial wet palette, such as *Masterson's Sta-Wet Palette* which features an airtight lid and is available in a variety of sizes. This palette is frequently used when mixing paint colors that you want to save for future use.

BRUSHES

A brush consists of three parts: a handle, which may be made of painted wood or acrylic; a metal ferrule, which connects the handle to the brush hair and holds it in a specific shape, and the synthetic filament or hair. Brushes are available in a wide range of sizes and styles. They make marks related to the brush shape: flat shader, angle shader, filbert, round, liner, script liner, wash/glaze, rake/comb, deerfoot stippler, mop, fan blender, etc. Brush names may indicate specific functions in applying paint. The chart opposite gives a description of the most commonly used brushes, and the techniques for which they are best suited. At the top of the list are liners, rounds, and flats—all are essential for most painters.

For best results purchase good quality brushes. Brushes for acrylics should have synthetic filament that is both soft and resilient. The brush should retain its shape, including a chisel edge or point when wet and when filled with paint. The brush should rest in and become an extension of the hand. A tight grip causes hand fatigue and restricts free movement of the brush.

Brushes should be cleaned thoroughly after painting. Soap and water will clean a significant amount of paint from the brush. However, a good brush cleaner will prolong its life. To limit the amount of paint that could be drawn under the ferrule, begin by thoroughly soaking brushes in clean, shallow water for about 4–5 minutes before painting. This will

BRUSH SELECTOR CHART			
BRUSH TYPE	**DESCRIPTION**	**TECHNIQUE**	**SIZES**
Liner (Spotter) (Script Liner)	Round Ferrule Pointed Tip	Linework Lettering Strokework Outlining	# 18/0 – #2 # 0 – # 3
Round Brush (Pointed Round)	Round Ferrule Round/Pointed Tip	Strokework Linework Washes Colorbooking	# 3/0 – # 20
Deerfoot Stippler	Round Ferrule Round Wedge	Stippling Fur Texture/Foliage Stenciling	⅛" – ⅜"
Flat Brush (Chisel Blender) (Flat Shader)	Flat Ferrule Square End	Strokework Chisel Linework Wash Colorbooking Sideloading	# 1 – # 20
Angle Shader	Flat Ferrule Slanted End	Sideloading Chisel Linework Colorbooking Stroke Roses	⅛" – 1"
Mop Brush	Flat Ferrule Loose Oval	Softening Varnishing	¼" – ¾"
Filbert (Cat's Tongue)	Flat Ferrule Oval Shape End	Strokework Blending Feathers	# 2 – # 8
Fan Brush	Flat Ferrule Spread Hairs	Blending Texture	# 1 – # 3
Comb/Rake	Flat Ferrule Series of Liners	Texture Hair, Fur, Grass Wood Graining	¼" – ¾"
Wash/Glaze	Flat Ferrule Square End	Wash Varnish	½" – 1"

saturate the hair under the ferrule, making it less inclined to draw paint. Place brush cleaner on the palette and work the brush back and forth through the cleaner. Rinse in running water. Shape the brush and dry flat to prevent any remaining paint particles from collecting under the ferrule. Store upright when the brush is completely dry.

WATER BASIN

You will need a container for holding water; paint must be cleaned from the brush frequently to prevent damage. Although a plastic bowl may be acceptable, you'll find that purchasing a divided water basin is well worth the investment. Clean water should always be available in one section. Fill the basin sections with shallow water no deeper than the hair of a flat or angle brush. This shallow level allows the brush to absorb water under the ferrule by capillary action rather than by saturation.

4

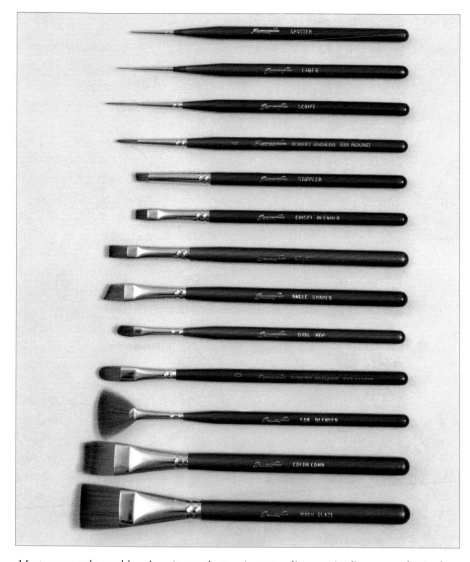

Most commonly used brushes: (top to bottom) spotter, liner, script liner, round, stippler, chisel blender, shader, angle shader, oval mop, filbert, fan, comb, and wash/glaze.

Tools for preparing wood surfaces before painting: (left to right) lint-free cloth, wood project, foam brush, sealer, wood filler, sanding blocks and sandpaper.

Soaking brushes in the basin can cause damage to the handle if the water is deep. *Never* soak brushes in dirty water.

To clean paint from the brush in the brush basin, place the hair in the ditch between the cleaning grid and the wall of the basin. Lean the brush into the shoulder of the cleaning grid. Tap only the ferrule against the grid, never the hair of the brush. The vibration in the metal ferrule will effectively remove paint from the brush. Brushing the hair over the grid will break the hair and damage the brush.

To clean the basin, fill it with hot water and add one tablespoon of dishwasher detergent. Microwave for ten minutes. Use a nylon scrubbing pad to remove any stubborn paint. Another method is to fill the basin with rubbing alcohol and allow to soak overnight.

PREPARING WOOD SURFACES

From small simple cutout shapes to large furniture pieces, wood is perhaps the most popular surface for decorative painting. However almost any surface is suitable (see page 6). A finished painting will look better on a smooth, blemish-free surface. Select wood that is free of knotholes and sanded as smooth as possible. Sanding equipment is a necessary part of preparation supplies. It is available in various grits (150–600 grits) and can be used for hand sanding or in a palm or orbital sander. Sanding blocks and files (for artificial nails) and oval sanding pads are easy to hold while sanding.

Remove any hardware prior to preparing the surface. Store all the pieces in a small plastic bag with a note as to which surface they belong. Sand the surface. Fill holes (except screw holes for hardware), nicks, dents, open-end grain and other flaws with wood filler. Since wood fillers shrink when dry, over-fill the holes and then sand smooth to the surface when the filler is dry. Wipe the dust from the surface using a lint-free cloth such as a microfiber towel, electro-

PAINTING ON VARIOUS SURFACES

Most any surface can be painted if prepared properly and appropriate paints and mediums are used. In addition to wood, other excellent surfaces for decorative painting are metal, porcelain, terra cotta, candles, fabric, and paper. Read product labels for usage guidelines.

Metal. Remove rust from old tin using naval jelly. Wash thoroughly with soap and water. Rinse with 1:1 white vinegar and water solution to remove any oil or residue. Seal with a spray or brush-on metal primer to improve paint adherence. Spray products should be used outdoors and often require two applications (allow 24 hours between coats). Spray evenly using thin coats to prevent drips.

Basecoat with a dry sponge brush using 1:1 paint and sealer for the first coat. This mixture will improve the bonding process. Allow 24 hours cure time before applying the second coat of paint only. When the design is finished, use a finishing spray for a smooth surface. Metal looks best without any brush marks.

Porcelain. Sand lightly if needed. Seal with a brush-on sealer, or mist with a matte finishing spray. Sealing improves the bonding. Transfer the design using *Super Chacopaper* which allows for easy removal. Since porcelain is such a beautiful surface, use transparent washes or sideloaded color to define areas of the design. Finish with several coats of varnish.

Terra Cotta. Terra cotta is very inexpensive and makes a good practice surface. Seal the inside as well as the outside of terra cotta pots to prevent water damage. Terra cotta is very porous and sealing will make basecoating easier. Basecoat both the inside and outside using several coats for solid coverage. When the painting has cure dried, varnish with 4–6 coats of polyurethane both inside and out. Allow the varnish several days to cure before planting. Painted pots should be used indoors. Terra cotta projects intended for outdoor use will require outdoor paints and finishes.

Candles. Clean candles with rubbing alcohol and an old nylon stocking. Alcohol softens the surface allowing the paint to adhere better. The nylon works as sandpaper to smooth the surface and remove mold release from the surface. Apply *DecoArt Candle Painting Medium* to the surface while it is still soft from the alcohol. Candle medium should be mixed in equal parts with acrylic paint to prevent the paint from separating on the waxy surface. The paint may be brushed or sponged on the candle. The entire candle may be basecoated to coordinate with other painted surfaces. A cosmetic sponge is ideal for sponging a basecoat. Transfer the design with *Super Chacopaper* and a stylus. Use very light pressure to prevent scoring the candle. To sideload color for shading and highlighting, use the medium on the back of the brush rather than

water. The medium can be used as a finish coat over the completed painting. Allow the paint and medium to cure 24–48 hours. Burn the candle until a depression forms that will accommodate a tea light. Tea lights can be replaced as needed in the painted candle.

Fabric/Canvas. Wash the fabric to remove sizing, then dry without using fabric softeners. Both can interfere with paint permanence. Wearable fabrics should be painted with fabric paint that remains soft and flexible. Canvas and heavy fabrics for decorative purpose can be painted with acrylics mixed with fabric medium. This mixture will be stiff. All paint should be heat-set with an iron when the painting is complete. The iron setting should be compatible with the fabric. Use a dry pressing cloth over the paint.

For lightweight fabrics, use a pencil to trace the design over a light-box or at a window. For heavy fabrics, trace the design onto a piece of tulle netting using a black *Sharpie* pen. Transfer designs with a .005 or .01 permanent ink pen. Brown ink blends well into most fabric painting. You may also transfer using *Super Chacopaper,* but avoid using graphite paper, which may mark your fabric.

When painting on fabric, fill an area with a smooth layer of paint. Blend shading and highlighting colors into the wet basecoat. Fabric brushes are stiffer than acrylic brushes so paint can be scrubbed into the fibers. Allow the first layer to tack up before placing additional shading and highlight colors. Rather than water, use the appropriate fabric medium, tipped on the back edge of the sideloaded brush. Blend slightly on the palette before painting.

Papier Mâché. Papier mâché is porous and should be sealed to eliminate extra basecoating. A layer of gesso will help smooth out any surface flaws. Sanding can also minimize rough areas. Papier mâché may be decoupaged with crinkled tissue or rice paper after basecoating to add interest to the surface. Since papier mâché is inexpensive, it is a good surface for practicing and experimenting. Use polyurethane for varnishing papier mâché boxes to prevent the lids from sticking.

Mat Board/Other Papers. Sealing paper surfaces makes it easier to clean up errors without damaging the surface. Sealing prevents the paper from absorbing paint quickly, so errors can be removed with a damp cotton swab. Apply the design with *Super Chacopaper,* water-soluble graphite, or white chalk paper. Areas may be filled with a wash of color or sideloaded directly on the background.

Pen and ink drawings are commonly done on paper surfaces. Seal the paper for painting after the inking has cured 24 hours. Use only permanent, waterproof inks. Use very transparent color when painting over inking.

static cloth (such as *Swiffer* disposable cloths), or a damp T-shirt.

Always sand and paint with the grain of the wood, not against it. Apply a water-based sealer over the entire surface including front, back, sides, and inside. Sealers stabilize the wood to prevent warping and help control moisture in the wood. Each manufacturer of acrylic paints makes a sealer that is formulated to its paint line. Avoid oil-based sealers. Other products to help mitigate surface flaws are available: commercial sanding sealers can fill gaps in extremely open grain, and tannin blockers help control seepage from small knots. Acrylic gesso can be used over the sealer to stop spurring (raised wood-grain caused by moisture from mediums and paints). Gesso has a very hard acrylic finish that further stabilizes wood. Furniture and boxes benefit from a coat of acrylic gesso applied as the first basecoat.

Paint the entire surface with solid color. Apply using thin layers of paint for better cure-drying between the layers. A dry sponge brush makes a smoother basecoat with thin layers of paint. Place a puddle of paint on the palette and work the paint into the sponge brush. Do not squirt paint directly onto the surface; it is difficult to judge exactly how much paint is needed. Too much paint on the surface or in the brush can create runs and drips on the edges.

Begin the basecoat in the center of the surface. Use a circular motion and scrub the paint into the wood grain out to the edges. Finish with a light stroke in the direction of the wood grain. Check for drips and smooth evenly. Allow each area to dry before painting the back and sides. Acrylic paint is dry when it feels warm and dry. It is still wet when it feels cool and damp. Acrylic paint must also cure-dry for 4–24 hours depending on temperature and humidity conditions. The surface will sand smoother if the paint is allowed to completely dry between

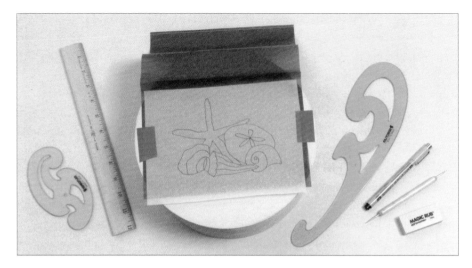

Tools for transferring your pattern include: (left to right) small French curve, ruler, tracing paper pattern taped over graphite paper using painter's tape, large French curve, fine-tip permanent pen, stylus, and eraser.

In addition to wood, decorative artists enjoy painting on a variety of surfaces: (left to right) terra cotta, paper, papier mâché, porcelain, candles, and metal (tin).

basecoats. Wipe the dust off from sanding before applying the next layer of paint. Repeat until the surface is a solid color. The last coat may be a wash of color to provide a little "tooth" to the surface. Mix about equal parts of paint and water for a final wash.

TRANSFERRING THE DESIGN

It's important to transfer the pattern accurately. Correcting a drawing while painting is difficult. The basic equipment for transferring include a .01 permanent ink pen, tracing paper, stylus and transfer paper. For projects painted with acrylics, transfer papers must be removable with water or with a soft eraser: water soluble graphites, *Super Chacopaper*, and white chalk paper are good choices.

Place the traced pattern on the surface and tape in place with painter's tape. Slip the transfer paper under the tracing. Check to make sure that the transfer side is down. Using the small end of the stylus, trace over the lines.

Drawing tools and guides can make

drawing and transfer more accurate. Use a ruler to draw straight lines. French curves are helpful for curved lines. A circle guide is imperative for drawing accurate circles. Trace only the parts of the design necessary for each step to avoid confusion. Apply details as needed.

BASECOATING THE DESIGN

After transferring the design, you're ready to paint. Many painters choose to fill areas of the design with solid basecoated colors. This is also referred to as color-booking. The color is always a middle value of the actual color of an object. Others apply only an even layer of color wash. Washes are useful over dark backgrounds to support the shading and highlighting colors. Some painters prefer to omit all area basecoating and simply apply the shading and highlighting colors over the background color.

Always soak the brush thoroughly before basecoating to reduce damage from paint. Squeeze out small amounts of paint and refresh the puddle as the paint is used. Load the brush by working the paint thoroughly into the hair. A properly loaded brush permits controlled release of the paint.

Base areas with an even layer of color. The edges should be crisp and clean and without any ridges. Begin in the center of an area and push the side of the brush into the outside line. The chisel end of the brush may leave an uneven edge. Use the largest brush that can be controlled in an area. Make shape-following strokes or strokes following the grain for more even basecoats. Allow each layer to thoroughly dry before applying another coat. Use thin layers of paint which will dry more thoroughly than a thick one.

It is easier to paint an area than to paint around an area. Paint underlying areas, those that are partial because they are under another area. Finish with areas that are whole and are, therefore, the top

elements in the design. To smooth out small ridges, use a small piece of brown paper bag for fine sanding when the paint is dry but still soft.

FINISHING

Once the decorative painting is complete, it is important to add a final finish. Clean up any errors and remove the remaining tracing lines with water or an eraser. Wipe the surface free of dust.

Varnishing is important not only for protection but also for enhancement of the paint colors. Select a large, soft brush at least 1" wide to use only for varnishing. The brush may be a synthetic flat brush or large mop brush. Use a damp, but not wet brush. It should carry a large amount of varnish without dripping. Place the brush flat on the surface and pull across slowly. The varnish should flow evenly from the brush. When the brush begins to drag, load with more varnish. Do not brush back and forth with the end of the brush as this causes the varnish to foam. Small bubbles will remain in the varnish from foaming. Check the edges to catch and smooth out any drips and runs.

Allow the varnish to thoroughly dry before adding another layer. After three coats, polish the varnish with 0000 steel wool or with extra-fine sandpaper (600 grit wet/dry). A mixture of dishwashing detergent and water serves as lubrication for polishing the surface. Dip the steel wool or sandpaper in the mixture and polish using a circular motion. Wipe clean with a damp cloth. Water will cause the surface to appear milky, but the varnish will clear as it dries. Apply another coat of varnish. The varnish may be polished after every coat or every other coat. Clean with soap and water and brush cleaner. Do not allow varnish to dry in the brush.

There are several types of varnish suitable for using with acrylics. For many

projects, interior varnish is a good choice. Generally, interior varnishes have a slight yellow tint which puts a warm glow to the finish. The varnish cures slowly and remains soft for some time. Varnishes are available in gloss, satin, and matte finishes. Use only one finish type. Do not mix finishes as they are not compatible. The most stable is gloss varnish which may be polished to a satin or matte finish. To retain the gloss finish, the final coat should not be polished. If using interior varnish on boxes, it is necessary to apply finishing wax to keep lids from sticking. Varnish all areas of the project with an equal number of coats to keep the surface stable. I recommend six coats of interior varnish—the more layers of varnish, the richer the colors in the painting. ***Note:*** *To serve food on finished surfaces, use a glass plate or paper doily.*

Exterior or polyurethane varnish creates a hard finish that can withstand sunlight and weather. It is available in matte, satin, and gloss finishes which should not be intermixed. Polyurethane varnish is clear so the colors in the design remain true. The varnish also has UV protection to help prevent colors from fading. The varnish dries and cures quickly. Finishing wax is not needed on lids or drawers as the varnish will not stick to itself. I recommend applying four coats of exterior varnish. On pieces to be used outside, finish the surface with paste wax. The wax will fill any small flaws in the finish and prevent cracks from developing in the finish. Once a year remove the old wax with ammonia and reapply the wax.

Spray finishes are best for dimensional pieces which can be difficult to varnish with a brush. Follow manufacturer's instructions for applying. Use several layers of light spray, then finish with several heavier coats. Avoid concentrated spray that creates runs or drips.

Acrylic Sideload

By Sharyn Binam, CDA, CCD, CPD

SIDELOADING IS ONE OF THE PRINCIPLE METHODS FOR APPLYING acrylics. A sideloaded brush has paint only on one side for placing graduated color. This technique is sometimes referred to as "floating color." And indeed, the paint should float on a layer of water in order to dry smoothly. Sideloads are used to place shading, highlighting and accent colors within the design. The contrast between light and dark values creates depth in the painting. Like other painting techniques, sideloading requires practice to master.

EQUIPMENT

The basic equipment for sideloading is a wet palette, brush basin, and various sizes of angle shaders. A helpful medium for softer sideloading is *Delta Color Float*. This water conditioner requires only one drop in each ounce of clean water used for sideloading. In breaking the surface tension of water it, in effect, makes water wetter. Acrylic paint chemically wants to dry flat and smooth. A film of water permits paint to float long enough to settle smooth.

Palette

A wet palette helps to balance water and paint in a sideloaded brush. The two fundamental aspects of sideloading are blending on the palette and placing color on the surface. They are of equal importance. All blending for the acrylic sideload takes place on the palette and care should be taken to blend well. I use a wet palette consisting of folded sheets of deli paper as described on page 3. Keep the palette wrinkle free for easier blending. Place small puddles of paint along the top edge of the palette.

About Sharyn Binam

Sharyn Binam's story will amaze and inspire all novice painters who are plagued with self-doubt and lack confidence in their abilities. When Sharon was a schoolgirl, a thoughtless (and mistaken) teacher proclaimed that she "had no artistic talent whatsoever," and should abandon hope of pursuing art. Crestfallen, she contented herself with helping her best friend schlepp artwork to class, but never really relinquished her dream of painting.

Years later—she recalls the exact date as June 15, 1984!—she summoned the gumption to take a beginner's painting class at a local craft store. It became a turning point in her life, as she discovered she had, indeed, a knack for decorative painting. Her artistic gifts have led her to a satisfying career as a designer.

Sharon is renowned for her southwestern, seashell, and floral designs, as well as her structured sideloading technique featured in her designs shown below. She paints only what comes from her heart, and ignores the rest. She advises other painters "Paint only what you love, but love what you paint," encouraging them to set aside their tyrannical self-criticism. She also emphasizes that nothing ensures success more than practicing strokework so "you control the brush, not the other way around."

With practice and persistence Sharyn became a Certified Decorative Artist in 1989, then a Certified Craft Designer (both through the Society of Craft Designers) and a Certified Professional Demonstrator (through the Hobby Industry Association). She's a member of the elite Delta Design Force (Delta Technical Coatings, Inc.) and on the Editorial Advisory Board for *Paintworks* magazine.

Sharyn teaches at national and regional painting conventions and at national and international seminars, and has authored 15 decorative painting books along with numerous magazine articles and pattern packets. Sharyn's newest book is her sixth southwestern book, *Desert Trails Volume 2*, which reflect the influences of her beloved Tucson, Arizona.

A resident of Tucson, Arizona, Sharyn Binam is well known for her southwestern designs (left), as well as her florals (below), and seashells.

Refresh small puddles frequently, rather than using a large puddle of paint. It is more difficult to work with tacky paint. Blending should be done on the remainder of the palette.

Since the palette keeps the paint from drying completely, you can blend in the same area (unless the color bleeds across the entire brush). Use a horizontal or vertical blending strip about 1" in length. Use pressure on the brush to keep the paint on the front, or "toe," of the brush. Blend slowly to control the brush and keep the palette tidy to avoid accidents.

Water Basin

Clean water is essential. Use a divided basin and fill the separate areas with shallow water no deeper than the hair of the brush. Add two drops of *Delta Color Float* to each section. Soak the brush well to thoroughly saturate all of the hair of the brush, including under the ferrule. If the back edge of the brush remains clean, rinsing the brush between sideloads is not necessary.

Angle Brush

Use an angle shader for sideloading. It consists of a long side (the front or toe of the brush), a short side (the back or heel of the brush), a chisel edge at the cut edge of the brush, and the flat or face of the brush. Tip the toe of the brush into the paint, keeping the back of the brush clean. Blend the color into the flat about ½ to ⅔ of the distance between the chisel and the brush ferrule. Blend the brush at the same angle as the hair is cut. To leave texture, paint with the chisel of the brush. To leave smooth color, use the flat of the brush.

Hold the brush with a relaxed grip. The brush should rest between the thumb and first two fingers. Fine movements of the brush are accomplished by rolling the brush between the thumb and forefinger. To paint with as much of the flat as possible, hold the brush at least 1" behind the ferrule. The angle brush is easy to maneuver from the flat to the chisel because the back of the brush is shorter. The flat makes smooth, graduated color and the chisel shapes accurate edges. All brushes require practice to master.

Clean the brush with soap and water and brush cleaner. Sideloading requires a sharp chisel on the brush for accuracy, so shape the chisel back into a sharp edge. A worn chisel produces a fuzzy edge. Dry your brushes flat and then store upright.

SIDELOADING COLOR

Wet the brush and squeeze out the excess drop against the edge of the basin. Hold the basin with the little finger to keep it from tipping while pressing firmly. Turn the toe of the brush down to carefully tip the paint onto the brush. The more paint used, the more difficult it is to control. The most common problem in sideloading is using too much paint.

Pick up a small touch of paint and blend on the palette 6–8 times. Rinse the brush only between colors or when the brush leaves a shadow mark from the back edge. This shadow mark indicates that the color has bled and the brush no longer has graduated color.

Sideloaded color or floated color is darker on the toe and fades to clean water on the heel of the brush. Begin each stroke or mark of the brush where the color will ultimately be the darkest. The most attractive color develops from several layers of sideloaded color. Transparent color creates luminosity in the painting and also makes small errors easy to fix or disguise.

There are several strokes used to create basic shapes of color. Natural shadows are a combination of wide and narrow widths of color. Avoid seeing only lines to shade against. Instead, look for the area between the lines.

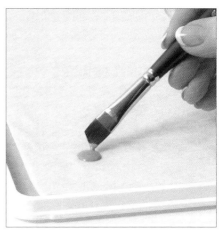

Turn the brush to accurately tip the brush with a small amount of paint.

Blend in a straight line about 1" to 1¼" to create graduated color on the brush.

Blend well using pressure on the brush for better control of the paint on the brush, palette, and surface.

Simply shading against a line, called outlining, creates no form or dimension.

CORRECTING ERRORS

Allow each layer to completely dry before painting another layer. From time to time you will want to correct a painting error. A common error is to place shading along one edge and highlighting along the opposite. Once the paint begins to settle on the surface, any disturbance will cause the paint to roll into a crusty edge. When the paint is still wet, errors can be wiped off with a damp cotton swab. Shadow lines can be omitted by adding clean water at the line of color.

Acrylic paint will flow where moisture allows, so do not paint next to an area that is still wet. If the flaw appears when the paint is dry, you can erase it with a pencil eraser dampened with saliva. A common problem is painting beyond the design lines. Clean up these ragged edges with the eraser method rather than sideloading the background color around the design. Use pencil replacement erasers with a sharp edge for accuracy.

The most common error is overpainting so that the color looks heavy or opaque. Learning to stop can be difficult. If the first shading color is well developed, it deters adding too much color. Build the shading through the second shading color then develop the highlights. Add the final shading in touches. After the first mark, all painting becomes adjustments and corrections until it looks right. The amount of contrast is a matter of personal perception and aesthetics.

BASIC STROKES

The strokes for placing sideloads are basic geometric shapes (see opposite). Creating wide and narrow color is the important consideration. The widest mark that any brush will make is when it is perpendicular to the line the color is placed against. For a narrow mark, use a smaller brush or pull the back of the brush closer to the line.

The toe follows the heel; the toe never leads the heel. Narrowing the angle of the brush to the line creates variations in the mark. The entire chisel edge of the brush begins and ends against a line. The back of the brush must close up any gaps in the placement of color. The strokes all conclude with finishing the brush into an edge.

To release extra water from the brush, use a "press and release" motion (a stroking pitty-pat). The brush should remain on the surface. To release more paint, increase the pressure applied to the brush. To release less paint, use less pressure on the brush. Although blending on the palette requires pressure to properly load the brush, placing the color is best accomplished with a soft touch.

It is easier to sideload a large brush; however, smaller brushes are easier to control. Consider the size of the area you are painting and choose your brush accordingly. For better control of the brush, pull towards yourself or your painting hand.

Position the surface for a clear view of the starting position, the area to be covered and the stopping point—you can't paint what you can't see! If right-handed, place the painting area to the left. If left-handed, place the work to the right. Use the practice sheet (opposite) to create the basic sideloading shapes: edge to edge, walking out, small triangle, right triangle, highlight pivot, tinting pivot, circular, crescent, and tornado.

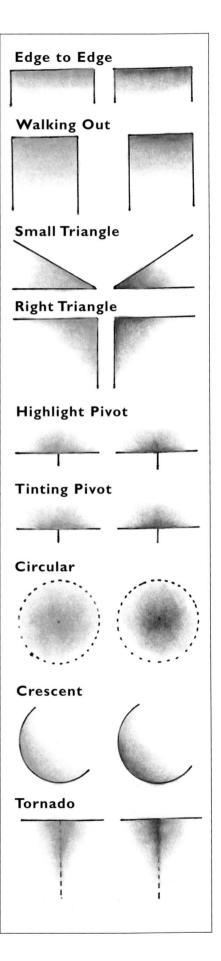

Edge to Edge

Walking Out

Small Triangle

Right Triangle

Highlight Pivot

Tinting Pivot

Circular

Crescent

Tornado

SIDELOADING PRACTICE SHEET

EDGE TO EDGE
Place the chisel along one edge keeping the brush perpendicular to the line. Paint on the flat of the brush and end on the chisel. Keep the edges crisp.

WALKING OUT
To walk out wide sideloaded color, place a series of edge to edge strokes. Each mark should be placed in the preceding mark before the color begins to lighten. Color should graduate.

SMALL TRIANGLE
Begin at the point of the triangle. Walk the color out between the slanted lines. Begin and end on the chisel edge but fill the area using the flat of the brush.

RIGHT TRIANGLE
Begin at the point of the triangle. Walk the color out within the right angle. Paint on the flat of the brush and lift to the chisel to taper the edges.

Use the right triangle to shape the pivot, circular and tornado strokes. The pivot is formed of two horizontal right triangles and the tornado is two vertical right triangles placed back to back. The circular stroke is four triangles placed back to back.

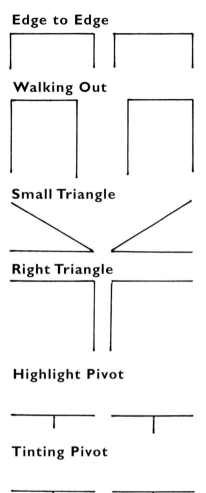

Edge to Edge

Walking Out

Small Triangle

Right Triangle

Highlight Pivot

Tinting Pivot

Circular

Crescent

Tornado

HIGHLIGHT PIVOT
Begin the mark at the center point of the line with the brush perpendicular to the line. Taper each right triangle into the side. Paint on the flat and pull to the chisel to finish.

TINTING PIVOT
Place the brush on the line with the toe pointed toward the center of the line. Pivot the heel over and around the toe. The brush heel turns 180°.

CIRCULAR
Place four right triangles around the center point. For better brush control turn the surface. The surface may be dampened to keep the paint open longer. Paint with light color and build up the color slowly.

CRESCENT
The color is widest at the center of the curve and tapers into both ends of the arch. Align the chisel with the line and pivot the heel over the toe on the flat. Finish into the line on the chisel.

TORNADO
Tornado strokes may be wide, narrow, long or short. The top along the edge is wide. The mark tapers into the center line forming a point. Color fades from the center line to each side. Dampen the area for longer open time. Avoid a hard line in the center.

Seashell Treasures

Designed by Sharyn Binam, CDA, CCD, CPD

MATERIALS

PALETTE

Delta Ceramcoat Acrylics:
Autumn Brown *~milk Choc.*
Burnt Umber
Dark Burnt Umber
Dark Flesh
Dunes Beige *– Cashmere Beigh*
Eggshell White *– Tapioca* *[White]*
Lichen Grey *– Barn Wood*
Light Ivory
Putty
Raw Linen *– Desert Sand + White*
Territorial Beige
Trail Tan
Western Sunset Yellow *– Sun flower*
White

BRUSHES

Robert Simmons Expression:
¼" and ⅜" angle shader: *Series E-57*
1" wash/glaze: *Series E-55*

SURFACE

Round-top card/trinket box #151-R
by *Sechtem's Wood Products*

OTHER SUPPLIES

See Basic Supplies, page 2
Fine sandpaper
Delta All-Purpose Sealer
Delta Color Float
1" sponge brush
Super Chacopaper (blue)
Old toothbrush
Delta Matte Exterior/Interior Varnish
0000 steel wool
Cable cord/chalk line #21 by *Lehigh*
Tacky glue (optional)

SOURCES

See page 127

INSTRUCTIONS

PREPARATION

Seal the box with *All-Purpose Sealer*. Sand to knock down the grain. Basecoat the exterior of the box with Eggshell White using three coats for solid coverage. Basecoat the interior of the box with Raw Linen.

Apply the design using *Super Chacopaper* and a stylus (see Transferring the Design, page 7). This transfer paper allows for easier removal of any lines still visible after painting. Make a paper copy of the design and cut out the areas of sand. Place this masking stencil over the design and tape in place. Thin Raw Linen slightly with water—the thinner the paint, the larger the spatters. Load the end of the toothbrush with thinned paint. Using a finger or brush handle, spatter within the stencil. Repeat the spattering using Trail Tan.

No area basecoats are used in this design. All color is applied in sideloaded, transparent layers.

PROCEDURE

Refer to the 4-step worksheet, page 17 and the shading placement diagrams, page 19 for guidance in placing colors accurately. Add *Delta Color Float* to your water. The first shading is indicated on the placement diagram with [:::::]. Apply the first shading color twice to create a good foundation for the other colors. Apply the details as indicated for each shell after the first shading. Place the second shading over the first, but in the smaller area marked with cross-hatching. The final shading or core dark is placed in basically triangular shapes in the areas marked with solid inking. Highlights are layered in the areas marked with [xXx]. Warm accent colors are indicated with [oOo] and cool accent colors with [/////].

Sand

Be sure the Raw Linen and Trail Tan spatter is dry, then shade with Raw Linen to fill any gaps between the sand and the shells. Deepen the shading with Trail Tan. Darken under the shells with Territorial Beige (see worksheet, page 17).

Sea Star

Shade the tip of each arm with Raw Linen. Taper the shading down the sides when painting the crescent stroke. Shade in the "V" shape between the arms and extend the shading toward the tips. Shade behind the sea biscuit. Place random-sized dots of Raw Linen down the length of each arm. When dry, deepen the shading with Trail Tan. Darken further with Territorial Beige. Highlight the center of each arm with Light Ivory and then with White. Add a warm accent of Dunes Beige to the edge of the arms, as indicated.

Sea Biscuit

Shade with Raw Linen at the ends of the center markings using crescent strokes; between the markings, use triangular strokes. For the outside edge, use triangular strokes. The color should be widest along the bottom and behind the snail. Deepen the shading with a mix of Raw

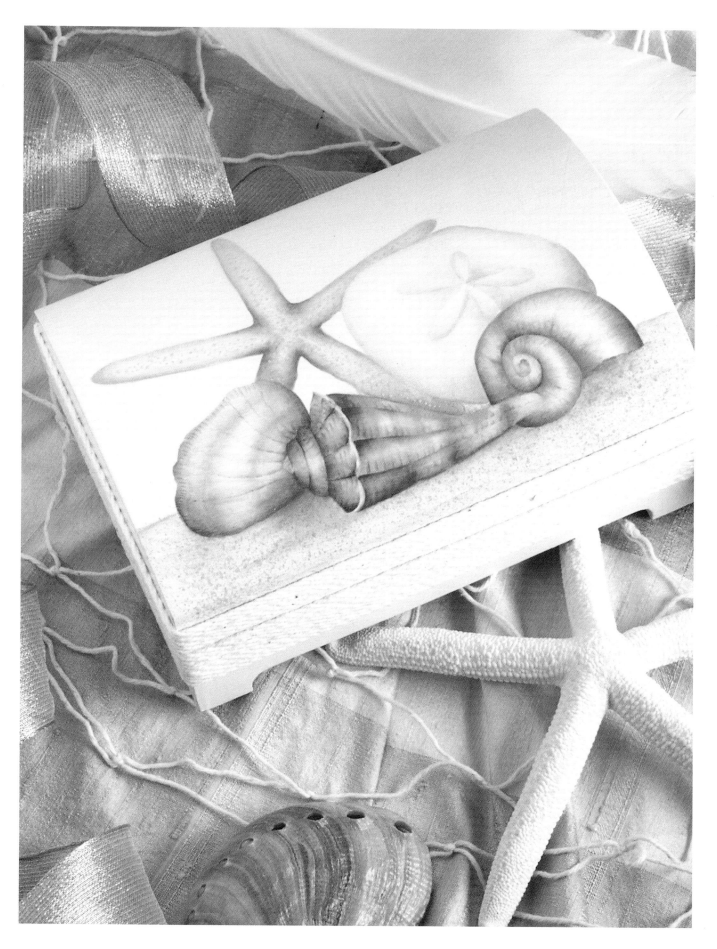

Linen and Lichen Grey. Darken further with Lichen Grey. Highlight the inside of the sea biscuit with Light Ivory and brighten with White. Add a warm accent of Dunes Beige to the edge.

Snail

Shade the inside and the outside edges of the curved shell with Western Sunset Yellow using triangular and crescent strokes. Sideload a ¼" angle brush with Dunes Beige and tap in the detail lines with the chisel edge of the brush. Deepen the shading with Territorial Beige. Darken further with Burnt Umber. Highlight through the center of the shell with Light Ivory and then with White. Add wide tornado-shaped strokes of Dark Flesh, following the direction of the detail lines. Add a cool accent of Lichen Grey to help recede some areas of the shell.

Whelk

Shade the many separations in the shell with Putty using triangular and crescent strokes. If the color is too light, add a touch of Dunes Beige to darken the Putty slightly. Sideload a ¼" angle brush with Territorial Beige and tap in the detail lines. Deepen the shading with Dunes Beige. Darken further with Dark Burnt Umber. Begin the highlight with Light Ivory placed in the center of the sections. Add the warm accent of Autumn Brown and the cool accent of Trail Tan or Lichen Grey using tornado strokes. Continue with another layer of Light Ivory and complete the highlight with White on the two center sections.

Venus Clam

Shade the edges of the clam with Western Sunset Yellow. The color should be wider on the sides of the shell. Sideload a ¼" angle brush with Territorial Beige and tap in long, curved lines through the shell and small lines

along the top edge with the chisel edge of the brush. Deepen the shading with Territorial Beige. Darken further with Autumn Brown. Highlight through the center of the shell with Light Ivory and then with White. Add warm stripes across the shell with Dunes Beige and then intensify with Dark Flesh.

FINISHING

The side of the box may be trimmed with cotton cording (*Lehigh #21 cable*

cord/chalk line found in hardware departments). Glue the cording in place with a clear-drying tacky glue.

Remove any remaining pattern lines with clean water on a brush. Wipe with a microfiber cloth to remove any lint. Varnish with 4–6 coats of *Delta Matte Exterior/Interior Varnish*. Allow each coat to dry thoroughly before applying the next. Polish with 0000 steel wool after the third coat and wipe clean with the cloth.

SEASHELL PAINTING CHART

AREA	SHADING	HIGHLIGHT	ACCENTS	DETAILS
Sand	1: Raw Linen			Raw Linen
	2: Trail Tan			Trail Tan
	3: Territorial Beige			
Sea Star	1: Raw Linen	Light Ivory	Dunes Beige	Raw Linen
	2: Trail Tan	White		
	3: Territorial Beige			
Sea Biscuit	1: Raw Linen	Light Ivory	Dunes Beige	
	2: Raw Linen + Lichen Grey	White		
	3: Lichen Grey			
Snail	1: Western Sunset Yellow	Light Ivory	Dark Flesh	Dunes Beige
	2: Territorial Beige	White	Lichen Grey	
	3: Burnt Umber			
Whelk	1: Putty	Light Ivory	Trail Tan or Lichen Grey	Territorial Beige
	2: Dunes Beige	White	Autumn Brown	
	3: Dark Burnt Umber			
Venus Clam	1: Western Sunset Yellow	Light Ivory	Dunes Beige	Territorial Beige
	2: Territorial Beige	White	Dark Flesh	
	3: Autumn Brown			

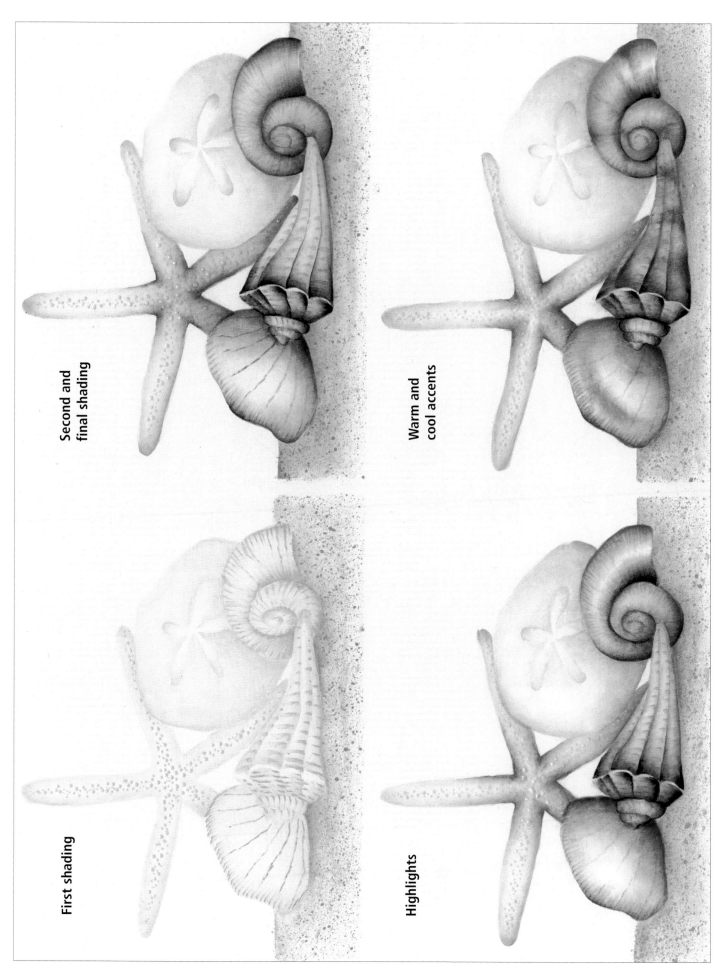

First shading

Second and
final shading

Highlights

Warm and
cool accents

17

SEASHELL TREASURES
PATTERN

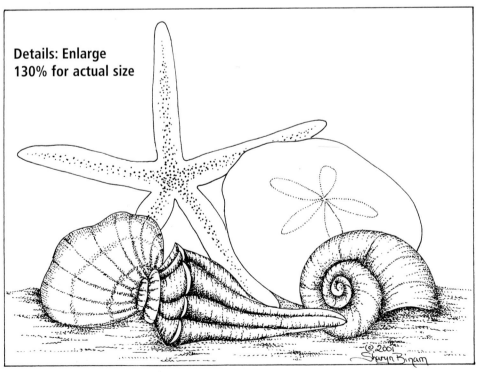

Details: Enlarge
130% for actual size

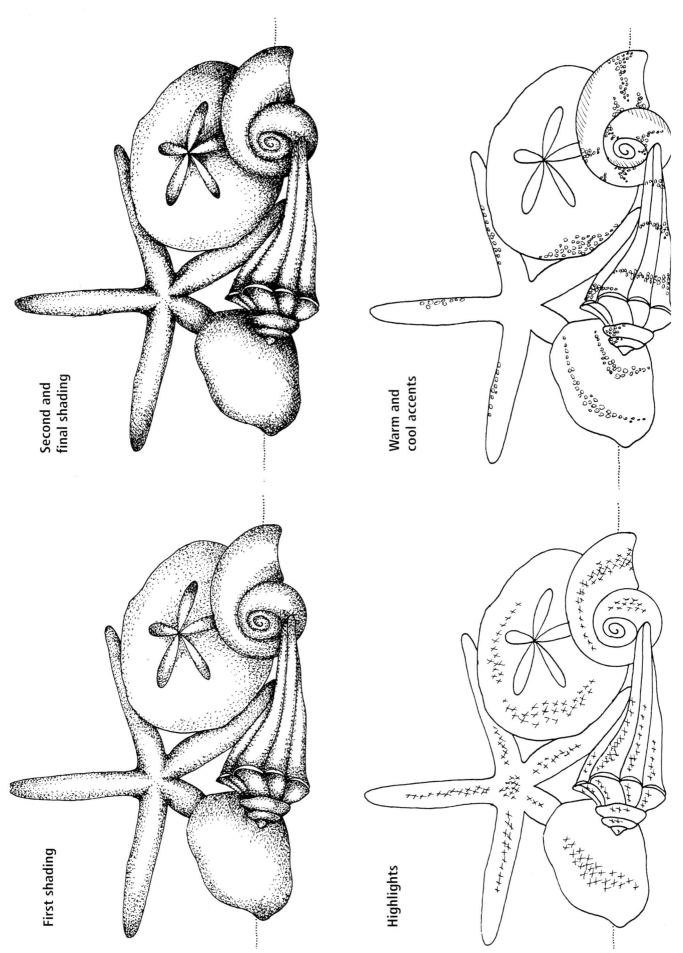

Second and
final shading

Warm and
cool accents

First shading

Highlights

19

About Debbie Cole

For Debbie Cole, decorative painting offers a refuge from the hectic pace of modern life. She believes that everyone has a creative gift, but that the busy-ness of our daily lives may obscure this gift and rob us of the relaxation and enjoyment of a creative pursuit. Debbie loved art since her childhood, but didn't pursue this love until her children were born. While working on her fine-arts major in college, she was frustrated because no one taught stroke techniques. She taught herself by reading as many decorative art books as possible.

Debbie's unique painting style, with its foundation in traditional techniques, employs a blend of floated color and dry brushing to achieve realism. She paints with multiple, thin layers to create very subtle changes. To achieve this, Debbie has created two lines of specialty brushes—one specifically for her dry-brushing technique and the other to replace a worn-out, old scruffy brush—perfect for the special fur technique on beloved teddy bears. She also loves to paint fruit, flowers, and still life. Debbie is a member of the Society of Decorative Artists and a Certified Decorative Artist. She teaches at the Society of Decorative Artists, Heart of Ohio Tole, and Creative Painting conventions. She travel-teaches across the United States, Canada, Japan, and Argentina. In addition to her own line of pattern packets, she has also published articles explaining her favored techniques, and her designs have been featured in numerous magazines.

Debbie's advice to painters who want to improve is to "slow down—you give in order to receive." By this she means give yourself the time to perfect your technique—even if only a few hours a week—and don't expect "instant" results. She always concludes her classes with this wish for her students: "May painting bring joy to your life!"

(above) "Fruit Medley" shows the forms completed (left) then with added glazes to create more depth and interest (right).
(right) "Autumn's Glory" appears flat (top) until glazes are added (bottom). Note the stippling technique on the large flower center and the small filler flowers.

$\mathscr{B}rush\ \mathscr{T}echniques$

By Debbie Cole, CDA

WHEN I BEGAN TEACHING REALISTIC ACRYLIC DESIGNS, I SAW THE NEED to make this style of painting easier for my students to learn. I developed some methods for creating the special techniques described in this chapter.

DRY BRUSHING

Dry brushing is a common technique that both acrylic and oil painters have been using for years. In general terms, it means to paint while using only a residue of paint in a brush. Different artists interpret this technique in a variety of ways; some use mediums or water in addition to paint. Other artists prefer painting with a completely dry brush, without water or mediums.

Since dry brushing is so easy to learn, I began using it to help my students apply shades and highlights on objects. Instead of having to walk out a float, which takes practice to master, the shade colors may be dry brushed. This method can also be used away from an edge, making the application of highlights much easier than applying a back-to-back float or a circular float. The best results are achieved when dry brushing is combined with floating. The first layer is an application of paint using the dry brushing technique. Then it is reinforced with a float of the same color, covering the same area. This process is continued until a smooth and even coverage of paint is created with each value applied.

The type of brush used during this technique is very important to the end result. Some artists use old scruffy brushes or round fabric brushes for this technique. I find that these do not work well for my style of painting. Because the scruffy is sometimes hard to control and the fabric brush tends to scratch the surface and/or creates lines in the paint application, I designed some brushes specifically for this technique. They have natural hairs that are soft enough to dry brush without scratching the surface, and they make it easier to apply the paint smoothly.

Before beginning to paint, it helps to condition the brush. Load the brush completely with *Delta Ceramcoat Gel Blending Medium*, working it thoroughly into the brush. Once the medium is worked into the hairs, remove as much as possible, leaving only a residue in the ferrule area. There should not be any residue in the hairs. The brush should feel dry to the touch. However, it is important that the medium is worked down into the ferrule so that the paint will not dry in the brush while painting. This also conditions the brush, so the hairs will not break while dry brushing.

To load the brush, first fill it completely with paint. Do not use any water in the brush while painting. Work the paint slightly into the hairs, so it is filled evenly. Then wipe the brush on a dry paper towel, keeping it at a 30° angle. It helps to hold the brush farther back on the handle to keep it at this angle. If this is difficult for you, keep your hand off the surface of the table in order to keep it lower. Use a lot of pressure while removing the paint, rotating the brush until only a residue of paint remains. It is important that the paint is removed evenly throughout the brush.

Place the brush on your surface where you want the greatest concentration of paint. Lay the brush back on its handle, keeping it at a 30 ° angle to the surface. It is important not to paint on the tip of the brush. Using light pressure, begin "scrubbing" the paint out of the brush in small circular or back and forth motions. Work the paint outward, allowing it to diminish so there is a gradation of color. Work slowly, so that the application is smooth and even. It is important to start with a light touch, slowly decreasing the pressure on the brush until you reach the outside edge of the area being painted. Sometimes it's necessary to repeat the application to attain the desired effect.

Diagram 1A shows an example of dry

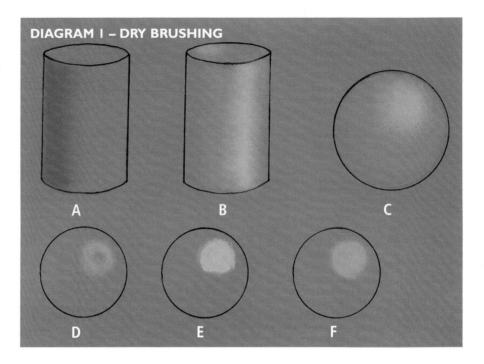

DIAGRAM 1 – DRY BRUSHING

A   B   C

D   E   F

brushing along an edge. Place the brush down next to the edge, using a back and forth motion as you slowly move away from the edge. Diagram 1B shows an example of painting highlights away from an edge. Place the brush at the top of the highlight area in the cylinder, then work slowly downward, using a back and forth motion. For the sphere (1C), place the brush in the center of the highlight area, then work slowly outward in a circular motion.

While dry brushing is an easy tech-

nique, there are a few common problems to watch for. It is important not to paint on the tip of the brush or to use too much pressure which may create a hole similar to that shown in 1D. The dry-brushed area will appear as a donut shape instead of a circular highlight. When too much paint is used, as in 1E, the highlight looks harsh and unnatural. Example 1F shows the results of applying the paint with no gradation. The same pressure was applied as far as the edge of the highlight, creating a harsh edge. This

For dry brushing, the brush should contain only a residue of paint. Lay the brush back at a 30° angle and apply slight pressure.

The example above shows the difference between a float of color and a glaze. The float (left in the photo) has some opaque color, while the glaze is completely transparent.

22

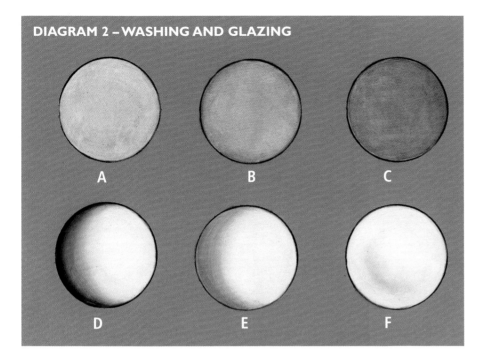

DIAGRAM 2 – WASHING AND GLAZING

A   B   C

D   E   F

same problem can result from using too much pressure while painting or getting water on the brush.

Because no water is used while painting, it is difficult to clean the brush between colors. To change from one color to another, wipe as much paint as possible onto a dry paper towel. Fill the brush again with gel blending medium and remove thoroughly. Load the new color into the brush, then wipe all from the brush. This should neutralize the previous color that was in the brush, allowing you to continue painting with the same brush. If the paint has built up and it must be cleaned, either wipe it on a *baby wipe* or rinse it in rubbing alcohol. Remember to wipe it on a dry paper towel until all the moisture is completely gone before resuming painting. At the end of a painting session, clean the brush in soap and water. I use a gentle soap, such as *Ivory* or *Pink Soap*. Reshape with a paper towel and lay flat to dry.

WASH OF COLOR

A wash of color is created by thinning paint to a semi-transparent to transparent consistency. This thinned paint is generally applied over an entire painting or an individual object within a painting. Sometimes it can be used to apply a background color to the bare wood, giving a *pickled* effect to the surface.

To create a wash, I find it useful to thin the paint with a combination of 75% water and 25% *Delta Color Float*. This helps the paint flow onto the surface with less streaking. The percentage of paint-to-water mixture will be determined by the type of wash desired. A light wash (Diagram 2A) would have very little paint mixed into the water mixture, while a medium (2B) or heavy wash (2C) would have more paint in the mixture.

Load the brush with the thinned paint, then blot it on a paper towel to eliminate puddles on the surface. Use as large a brush as you can control. Keeping the brush at a 30° angle helps the wash flow evenly out of the brush and prevents brush marks. Start at the top and work downward. Work quickly and do not stop painting unless you have reached an edge. It is important not to go over and over the same area as this will cause the wash to streak. In large areas,

dampen the entire surface lightly with the water mixture, then apply the wash. This will eliminate streaking, but the wash will require a little more paint. If necessary, repeat the wash, but be certain the first wash is completely dry before adding a second wash.

GLAZING COLOR

Glazing is also an application of semi-transparent to transparent color. However, its purpose is to add more dimension and interest to the painting. This technique is generally used to apply accents and/or to build greater values. It is different from a wash in that it covers isolated areas rather than entire objects within a painting.

To create a glaze, use as large a brush as possible. Corner-load the brush with a small amount of paint. This is similar to loading a brush as if to float. Stroke the brush back and forth on the palette, working the paint into the brush until it appears transparent. Apply as if walking out a float of color. Repeat if necessary. With each layer, the color becomes more vibrant. Refer to Diagram 2 for examples of a floated shade (2D), a glazed shade (2E), and a glazed accent (2F).

STIPPLING

Stippling is the act of "pouncing" a paint-filled brush up and down on a surface to create texture. This technique can create many types of texture, but is commonly used to create fur on animals and for foliage in landscapes. It may be completed with any brush, but generally a deerfoot or a scruffy brush is preferred. The effect will be different depending on the brush used. The correct amount of fresh paint, the brush pressure, and the amount of coverage are key elements to successful stippling.

To stipple using a scruffy brush, load the tips of the hairs lightly with paint. Pounce up and down on the palette

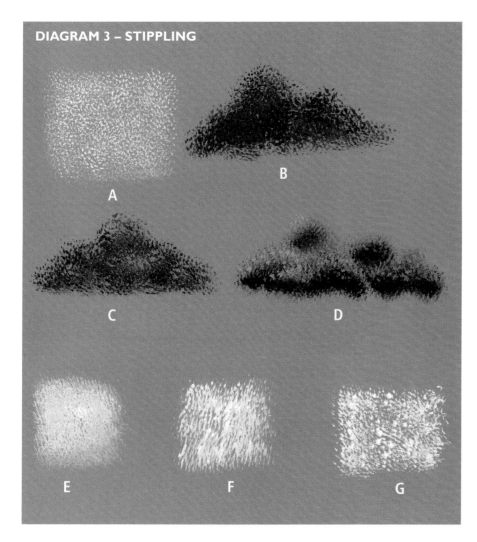

DIAGRAM 3 – STIPPLING

A

B

C

D

E

F

G

To stipple, hold the brush perpendicular to the surface, using very little pressure on the tips.

paper until a light texture is created. Hold the brush perpendicular to the surface while loading the brush and when stippling. Once the brush is loaded properly and is in the proper position, lightly pounce it on the painting surface. Use very little pressure. Too much pressure and/or too much paint will completely cover the area rather than create a texture. As you stipple, turn the brush with each pounce to avoid creating a pattern. Slightly overlap each pounce so that a smooth and even texture results. Do not rush the stippling process; take your time. If an area is missed from working too fast, it will make the stippled area look splotchy. Also, always be sure to use fresh paint when stippling. If the paint

begins to dry, a *skin* will form on the top of the paint. This will cause the stipple to get little clumps.

This light and airy style of stippling gives a light speckled texture. It can be used to create fur on a teddy bear, highlight or shade leaves on a tree top, and add texture to stoneware, etc.

The amount of pressure placed on the brush while pouncing up and down is very important. To create an open texture, use a very light touch (Diagram 3A). If too much pressure is used, the result will be an opaque coverage. The background color must show through to produce texture. There will be times when a heavier texture is desired, such as for foliage (3B). Use more pressure on

the brush while pouncing up and down. Even with this heavier application, the background color should still show through for the textural effect. Stipple highlights on foliage to give it dimension. This can be done with the brush loaded with a single highlight color as in 3C or double-loaded with two foliage colors as in 3D.

To use a deerfoot brush, load in a similar manner as the scruffy brush. Because of the unusual shape of this brush, it can be used in two different ways. It can be pounced using the broad, flat side or the edge that points outward. Both of these will create a heavier texture than the scruffy brush. Generally, the deerfoot is used for heavier coverage needed for tree tops and rust on rocks.

When stippling, some common problems to avoid are using too much pressure or too heavy of a coverage (3E). Dragging the brush or using an incorrect brush position will create streaking (3F). Using paint that has dried on the palette or brush will create clumps in the paint, giving an irregular texture (3G).

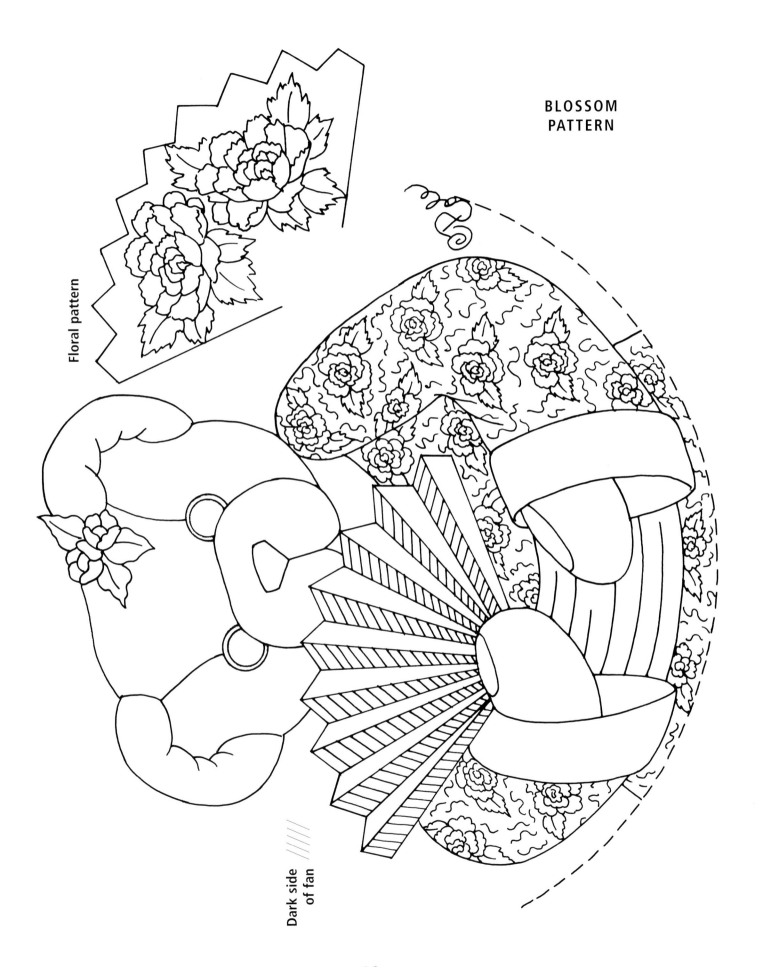

Floral pattern

BLOSSOM
PATTERN

Dark side
of fan

MATERIALS

PALETTE

Delta Ceramcoat Acrylics:

Black	Light Ivory
Black Green	Maple Sugar
Blue Storm	Old Parchment
Burnt Umber	Quaker Grey
Candy Bar Brown	Rain Grey
Chocolate Cherry	Raw Sienna
Coral	Spice Brown
Dark Night Blue	Spice Tan
Fiesta Pink	Tomato Spice
Forest Green	Wedgewood Green
Liberty Blue	

Delta Ceramcoat Gleams:
14K Gold

BRUSHES

Silver Brush Ltd.. Brushes: (available singly or in sets from the artist)

#0, #2, #4, #6, and #8 scruffy: *Cole Scruffy Series 2101S*

¾" and ½" square wash: *Golden Natural Series 2008S*

#6 shader: *Golden Natural Series 2002S*

#0–#8 rounds: *Cole Dry Brushes Series 2100S*

#00 liner: *Golden Natural Series 2007S*

SURFACE

12" diameter wooden plate with 8" diameter center by *Wayne's Woodenware*

OTHER SUPPLIES

See Basic Supplies, page 2
Ruler
Small sea sponge
Delta Ceramcoat Color Float
Delta Ceramcoat Gel Blending Medium
Delta Ceramcoat All Purpose Sealer
Delta Ceramcoat Matte Varnish

SOURCES

See page 127

Blossom

Designed by Debbie Cole, CDA

INSTRUCTIONS

PREPARATION

Sand, seal, and then sand the plate again. Undercoat the entire plate with Spice Tan. Trace the pattern on page 25 onto tracing paper and transfer to the plate (see Transferring the Design, page 7). Use a ruler when transferring the straight lines on the fan.

BASECOATS

Basecoat the background area and between the rims with Dark Night Blue. When dry, add the texture to the outer circle of the plate, using a dampened small sea sponge loaded with Tomato Spice. Pounce the sponge up and down lightly. Use the clean side of the sponge to soften the texture. Repeat this step using *Gleams* 14K Gold.

Basecoat the rims and back of the plate with Candy Bar Brown + Tomato Spice (1:1). The kimono and flowers on the bear's head are Tomato Spice. The bear remains the Spice Tan undercoat color. Basecoat the fan with two colors. The light sections of the fan are Maple Sugar; add a line of Maple Sugar + Old Parchment (1:1) to the left sides of these sections. The dark sections of the fan are Spice Tan; add a line of Raw Sienna to the left sides of these sections.

Transfer the floral pattern onto the fan. Outline all the pattern lines with thinned Raw Sienna.

Basecoat the collar, cuffs, and kimono sash with Black. Flower leaves on the bear's head are Forest Green. Line the details of the bear's face with Spice

Brown, then basecoat the iris of the eyes with Spice Brown, and the pupils with Black. The nose is Candy Bar Brown.

PAINTING DIRECTIONS

Mixing paint. When mixing paint, follow the ratio of paint listed just like a recipe. The first number represents how many parts of the first color listed, the second number represents the second color, and so on. Use an equal measurement, such as one drop or the tip of a palette knife to measure each part. Allow each drop time to spread on the palette paper to judge its size before adding another drop.

Bear's Head and Paws

Dry brush Maple Sugar + Spice Tan (4:1), for the highlights on the bear. For placement, refer to the Highlight Diagram on page 28. Use a round brush, varying the size in accordance with the area being painted. Repeat these highlights until a smooth and even coverage of paint is created (see Step 1 photo, page 29).

Float Raw Sienna + Spice Brown (4:1) to shade the bear, walking out the float where necessary. For placement, refer to the Shading Diagram on page 28. Reinforce the shades with Spice Brown, covering a smaller area.

Stippling. The stippling colors from dark to light are Spice Tan, Maple Sugar + Spice Tan (1:1), and Maple Sugar. Using a scruffy brush, begin adding texture by stippling very lightly (see Step 2 photo). Apply the color one value lighter than the area being worked.

For example, in the dark areas, use

Spice Tan. In the highlight areas, use Maple Sugar.

Fur Texture. Using a #00 liner brush and thinned paint, add small, short hairs to the fur. Just as in stippling, the lines should be one value lighter than the area being worked. The colors used from dark to light are Maple Sugar + Spice Tan (1:1), Maple Sugar, Maple Sugar + Old Parchment (1:1), and Old Parchment. Thin the paint to a cream-like consistency. Work one area of the bear at a time. Start in the middle of an area and work outward, pulling short lines that are approximately ⅛" long. When the fur is complete, apply a light wash of Raw Sienna.

Glazing the Fur. To glaze, load the brush with a minute amount of paint. Stroke the brush back and forth on the palette paper until most of the paint is out of the brush. What remains is a transparent color. Apply as if walking out a float of color. Repeat if necessary. With each layer, the color becomes more vibrant.

Glaze the dark areas of the bear again, using Burnt Umber. Then glaze Dark Night Blue only in the darkest areas of the bear. Add a rosy blush to areas of the fur by glazing with Tomato Spice, referring to the oval areas marked "A" on the highlight diagram below.

Eyes. Line the perimeter of the iris with Black. Float Rain Grey on both edges of the pupils. When dry, place three or four small dot glints in the center with Quaker Grey. Add star-shaped lines of Quaker Grey in the upper left corner of the pupil. Place the final glint with a dot of Light Ivory.

Nose. Shade the nose with Chocolate Cherry. Highlight with Spice Tan + Candy Bar Brown (1:1), reinforcing with Maple Sugar.

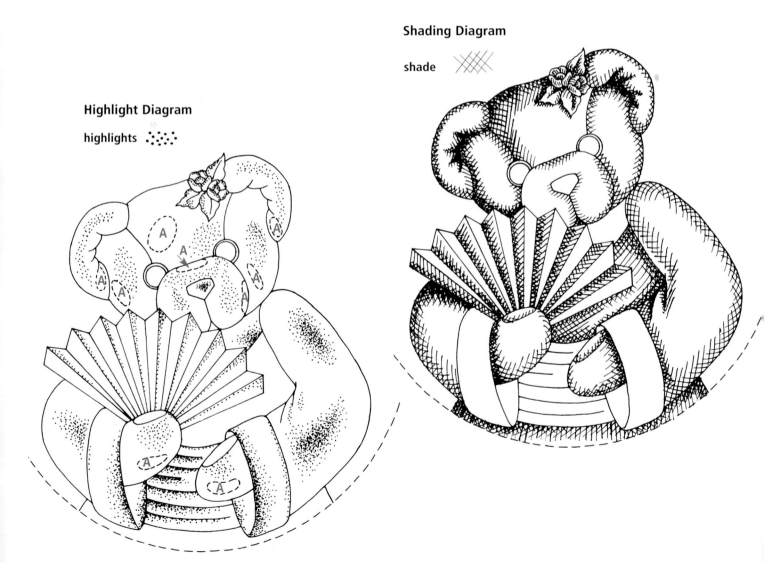

Highlight Diagram

highlights

Shading Diagram

shade

Kimono and Flowers on Head

Float the first shades with Candy Bar Brown. Dry brush the highlights on the kimono and float the flowers with Fiesta Pink. Keep these floats very soft by working them on your palette paper. Float the second shades with Chocolate Cherry. Add the second highlight with Fiesta Pink + Coral (3:1), in the same manner as the first. Transfer the rose pattern to the kimono. Outline the pattern with *Gleams* 14K Gold using a #00 liner. Glaze the darkest areas of the kimono with Black.

Sash, Cuffs, and Collar

Float Blue Storm to highlight. Reinforce these areas with a second highlight of Liberty Blue. Add a final glint of Liberty Blue + Light Ivory (5:1). Glaze Black in the darkest areas, going right over the highlights.

Leaves

Float to highlight with Wedgewood Green + Forest Green (1:1). Float to shade with Forest Green + Black Green (3:1). Glaze the darkest areas with Black Green.

Fan

Wash the flowers with Tomato Spice and the leaves with Raw Sienna. When dry, wash the leaves a second time with *Gleams* 14K Gold. Glaze the dark sides with Burnt Umber and the light sides with Maple Sugar + Old Parchment (1:1). Glaze the darkest areas only with Chocolate Cherry.

FINISHING

Allow 24 hours to cure. Varnish with at least two coats of water-based varnish, following the manufacturer's instructions.

(below) Basic strokework facilitates the building of many exciting shapes and wonderful pieces of art. The painted pieces shown use no more than what is described in this chapter.

(below, right) "Setters a.m." by Heather Redick, a limited-edition print.

About Heather Redick

Mastering old-world techniques to perfection, Heather Redick loves to pass along her expertise, declaring that her greatest joy comes from teaching—"showing students how to achieve beautiful, rhythmic stokes." Initially self taught, she studied with Priscilla Hauser and Russian masters Larisa Dyatlova and Boris Grafov. Heather now specializes in Zhostovo-style florals.

In 1990 Heather opened a decorative-art retail store and began giving lessons, teaching mainly her own designs in both oils and acrylics. She achieved certification with the Society of Decorative Painters with her first submission in 1992. Her business grew and in 1995 she developed a mail-order catalog, assembling a host of pattern packets and participating in her first trade show. In 1996, she began travel-teaching and offering seminars for stores, small studios, and conventions throughout Canada, the United States, Japan, Malaysia, Singapore, Australia and Taiwan. She has even conducted painting lessons via the Internet.

Heather's design books include *Zhostovo Florals, Holiday Tree Ornaments, Folk Flowers, Elegant Egg, Blue & White*, and most recently *Mastering Strokework*, as well as a book based on an Anne of Green Gables theme. She has also authored technique books, DVDs, and videos and self-designed over 80 "how to" decorative art instructional packets. Her business includes her own wood manufacturing shop which produces many original wood surfaces for her projects. Heather has perfected a line of quality liner brushes for the exquisite techniques she loves so much.

Heather lives in the small Canadian village of Zurich, Ontario, Canada. Her supportive family (husband, daughter, and son) not only help her with her work, but also provide laps for her English Setters, which Heather breeds and shows as a hobby. She has immortalized two of them in her first limited-edition print, entitled "Setters a.m." (shown below).

Strokework

By Heather Redick, CDA

STROKES ARE ANY "MARKS" APPLIED WITH YOUR BRUSH AND PAINT, to any surface, to fill a predetermined shape. Strokes can work alone, and in unison with other strokes. Strokes can be separate or overlapped, finished or unfinished. Strokework is, for me, the ability to control the brush.

Using my definition, this means that painting excellent strokework will enable you to successfully achieve a high level of painting skill, regardless of style. Controlled strokes are achieved by understanding how to direct and manipulate your brush and media in relationship to the painting surface. Every angle change, every pressure change, or every motion change will produce a different impression or mark on your piece.

BEFORE YOU BEGIN

Choose your surface. Decorative painters can paint on anything from wood, paper, glass, plastic, wax, and fabric to just about anything that is stationary. These surfaces have varying textures and may be rough, smooth, slick, porous, non-porous, or absorbent. The surface and choice of painting style will influence your selection of media, which also includes the paint consistency, paint opaqueness, the amount of paint in your brush, and the type of brush. For example, you cannot paint magnificent strokes on an unsealed, porous surface with a brush loaded in the same manner that it would be for use on a sealed, slick surface. If you practice, do so on a surface similar to and prepared in the same manner as that on which you intend to paint.

Choose your medium. You have a wide choice of mediums to choose from including oils, watercolor, acrylic, etc. Paints come in a wide variety of pigment/color, quality, opaqueness, transparency, and consistency, and a range of drying options. Depending on your choice, you may need to alter the paint to suit the surface and style of design. For example, you would not want to use a thin consistency of paint if you are painting opaque strokes on a sealed, slick surface.

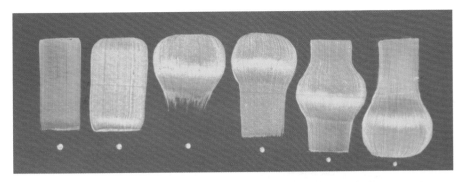

Fig. 1. Variations of a basic flat stroke, both finished and unfinished, shown with pressure changes within the stroke.

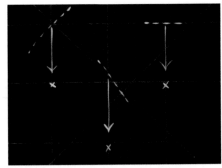

Fig. 2. Mark the destination. Determine the beginning angle of the chisel. Move to the spot.

Choose your brushes. Some brushes are made of a synthetic fiber. Within this category, there are many different formulas, resulting in a variety of performance. Some brushes are totally natural fiber. Again, these fibers vary, and the performance of each is different. This category includes Red Sable, Kolinsky, Squirrel, Pony Hair, etc. A third type of brush uses a combination of synthetic and natural fiber. Depending on the formulas used in the manufacturing, you will again experience different effects from a variety of brushes. They are your most valuable painting tool and greatly influence the proficiency of your strokework.

Loading your brush. If you are working with acrylic paints, invest in a *Masterson's Sta-Wet Palette.* Use the paper that comes with the palette; it's so important to load your brush on a surface that is conducive to pushing paint into the brush. The matte texture of the paper will allow you to blend and work with your paint. As you press on the paper/sponge, an indentation or pool is created helping to control the paint from spreading out to the sides or edges of the brush. You are able to easily control the paint consistency on this palette.

There are a variety of ways to load your brush depending on the desired outcome, but for almost all applications *evenly* should be a constant. Evenly means that each and every hair in the brush should be surrounded by an equal amount of paint. Sometimes this will mean surrounded by a lot of paint; other times it may mean surrounded by very little paint.

In order to load your brush evenly, approach your palette with your brush upright. Pull paint from the outside edge of the puddle, a little at a time, filling your brush with the desired amount of paint. Move to a separate spot on the palette, and blend the paint equally/evenly through your brush. If you have too much paint in the brush, gently wipe on a soft, absorbent towel, and then re-coat the outside hairs with a small amount of paint. If you need to moisten your brush, touch your water, touch your towel, and re-blend on your palette.

You need to make the paint consistency a priority concern if you want to develop your strokework. The longer and finer the stroke, usually means a thinner consistency. For shorter or textured strokes, the paint needs to be creamier. For blended strokes, use a bulkier consistency.

THE BASIC FLAT STROKE

Strokes come in every shape and size. To develop your stroke skills, begin by understanding a very basic flat stroke. Once you understand the importance of each step in this beginning stroke, you can move forward to produce a multitude of variations, at the same time advancing your painting skill level dramatically. You should be able to see and feel all aspects within each stroke, and then move to improve any deficiencies (Fig. 1).

• Attention to the preparation of your surface, media, brushes, and how you load them, will impact the results you attain. The paint consistency for practicing should be creamy, not too thin or too thick. The amount of paint in your brush should be substantial.

• Break all strokes down into as many steps as you can. Allow each step the same importance. Concentrate on painting with "rhythm," giving each step within one stroke the same "beat."

• Before you begin you must first know where the stroke will end. Knowing where you must end will influence how you begin. Position yourself to allow for free extension of your arms (Fig. 2).

• Strokes move more gracefully if you avoid the use of your wrists and fingers. Use your hands and fingers to hold the brush securely and concentrate on moving your arms to guide the brush. Students who use their small finger to control their hands sometimes have a tendency to lean the brush. Bracing yourself is important but must not interfere with your ability to keep the brush upright or to execute a variety of "leans" needed for different stroke applications.

- Approach your palette and your work with your brush at a right angle to the surface.

- Turn your work as you paint so that you can approach each stroke comfortably and from a good visible vantage point.

- You can "pull" the stroke towards yourself, or "pull" the stroke away from yourself. The important thing is to see and to watch each and every hair as you move through the stroke.

- Learn to paint with different brush styles and sizes.

- Brush recommendation: ¾" flat wash by *Robert Simmons Expression* or *Sienna.*

Flat Brush/One Color

There are four steps, or beats, to this stroke (touch, then begin to move and pull the stroke, come to a stop, and finally lift) (Fig. 3).

First, begin by marking a spot where the stroke will end, then determine a starting point. Touch the surface with the "chisel" edge of the brush. The chisel is at a right angle to the direction of the stroke. *Note: in order to be on the chisel edge, the brush must be upright.*

Secondly, pull the stroke while maintaining the upright position. Pull this stroke, do not apply any pressure, but move slowly and directly to the spot. The width of the stroke should be the same from beginning to end. Thirdly, stop still in the upright position. Lastly, lift up and off without moving or bending your wrist or fingers.

If your brush is not loaded evenly, you will see variations in the color or streaks, or perhaps run out of paint before arriving at your destination. Understanding the four steps is very important before advancing to variations of this stroke. By adding or subtracting steps or beats we begin to understand how to manipulate the brush.

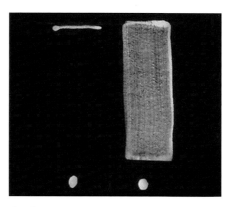

Fig. 3. Touch. Pull the stroke with no pressure.

Pressure applied at the beginning or end, or anywhere in-between the steps will change the stroke substantially. With the addition of pressure comes an increase in the difficulty. Controlling how much pressure and carefully positioning the pressure requires concentration. Pressure can vary. It may be constant throughout, or used only at the beginning, middle or end of a stroke.

Apply constant pressure. The format is similar to that of the first stroke example. Touch the surface to begin. Apply pressure. A slight lean of the brush in the direction the stroke is moving may be needed. The amount of pressure applied and the potential of the brush will determine the width of the stroke (Fig. 4).

Pull the stroke. The stroke is pulled maintaining equal pressure until reaching its destination. Stop and relieve pressure. The hairs of the brush should move back to their original shape. Lastly, lift up and off the surface.

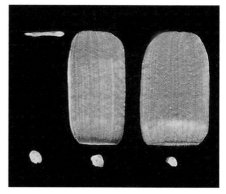

Fig. 4. Touch. Apply pressure and pull the stroke.

Applying and releasing pressure between different steps.

Pressure at the beginning of the stroke (Fig. 5A). Touch. Apply pressure/move/release pressure. The brush leans slightly in the direction of the stroke as pressure is applied. Slowly begin to move through the stroke. The hairs of the brush continue to move and expand as pressure is applied. As the stroke gains a rounded top (ball shape), the pressure is released slowing moving to create a "ball" at which point the hairs have re-grouped and the brush is back up on the chisel edge. Pull the stroke in the same manner as the first example. Stop. Lift.

Pressure in the center of the stroke (Fig. 5B). Touch. Pull. Apply pressure/move/release pressure. The "ball" is created in the center of the stroke. Pull the stroke. Stop. Lift.

Pressure at the end of the stroke (Fig. 5C). Touch. Pull. Apply pressure/move/release pressure. The "ball" is created at the end of the stroke. Stop. Lift.

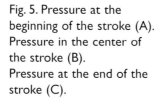

Fig. 5. Pressure at the beginning of the stroke (A). Pressure in the center of the stroke (B). Pressure at the end of the stroke (C).

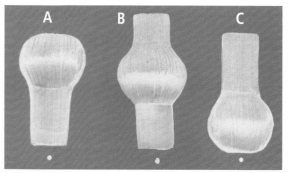

Being able to see the hairs expand and relax is key to successfully completing these strokes.

Variation of above. A variation can be done with and without pressure to create a very different mark. The stroke begins in the the same way as those in examples 5B and 5C. Touch; then pull and "wisp" off of the stroke. (Picture an airplane leaving the runway.) Your arm moves through the stroke lifting gradually leaving a frayed end on the stroke.

Pressure can be applied at any point in the stroke (Figs. 6A–C). Paint in a methodical, step-by-step rhythmic manner. Analyze the smallest of details.

Changing Chisel Angle

For all of the previous examples the chisel edge of the brush was placed at right angles to the direction (or spot) that the stroke was headed. Controlling these same strokes with a variety of changes to the angle or direction of the chisel creates a new challenge. The steps within the stroke require considerably more control.

Drawing a number of lines in the direction the strokes are to be pulled helps to keep the stroke moving in the right direction.

Chisel angle changes at the beginning of the stroke. The steps in these strokes are identical to the four steps in the first example. Touch; pull the stroke; stop; lift. The first stroke is a basic flat stroke with the chisel edge of the brush at right angles to the direction of the stroke.

The second stroke begins at an angle of about one o'clock. The following strokes show the angle increasing until the chisel is in line with the destination. Continuing to change the angle will result in a final stroke similar to the first (Fig. 7).

Mastering this and the previous

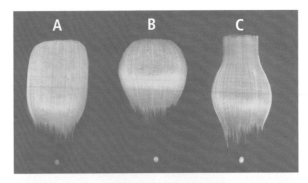

Fig. 6. Flat with pressure, wisped end (A).
Flat with pressure, wisped end (B).
Flat with pressure at the end, wisped (C).

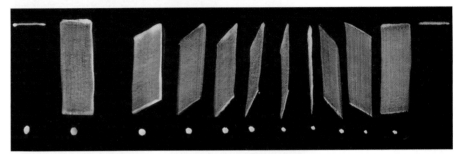

(above) Fig. 7. Basic flat strokes pulled with the chisel at different angles.
(far left) Fig 8. Basic flat stroke varying the beginning angle of the chisel and different pressure applications.
(left) Fig. 9. Variety of comma strokes.

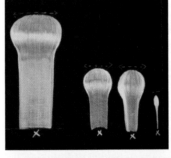

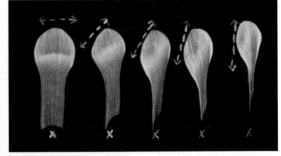

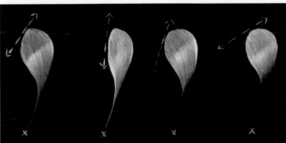

(above, left) Fig. 10. Basic flat strokes with pressure at the beginning.
(above) Fig 11. Basic flat strokes with pressure at the beginning, and changing the beginning angle of the chisel edge of the brush.
(left) Fig. 12. Comma strokes beginning on different angles, both finished and unfinished.

examples prepares us for another level of brush control. Combining pressure changes with changes of the chisel angle produces variations (Fig. 8) that, when mastered, will make comma strokes and "S" strokes (those strokes most familiar to decorative painters) simple tasks (Fig. 9).

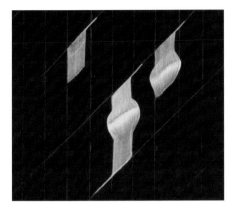

Fig. 13. Motion of "S" stroke.

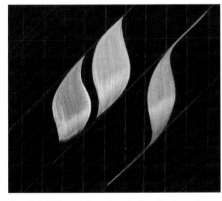

Fig 14. "S" strokes, both finished and unfinished.

COMMA STROKES

Comma strokes are wonderful, beautiful strokes that can be executed in a variety of ways, with a variety of brushes to fill so many shapes. Some are fat, others are thin, some short, some long, some rather curved, and others quite straight. They may have fine long tails, or short wisped-off tails, or tails that fall somewhere in-between. The shape and finish of the stroke is dependent on the style and design you are working with and the shape to be filled (Fig. 9).

A basic flat stroke with the pressure or ball shape at the beginning of the stroke (with changes to the angle of the chisel) requires the same control that is needed to execute a comma stroke (Figs. 10 and 11).

Determine the angle of your chisel. Touch; press into the stroke, leaning the brush slightly to the side, in the direction of the stroke. Pull slowly, without turning or changing the angle of the brush, releasing pressure. Time must be allotted for the brush hairs to reform. Finish the stroke slowly on the chisel edge of the brush. Some strokes will be unfinished depending on the style of painting (Fig. 12).

"S" STROKES

Like commas, these strokes are useful for filling in many shapes. A basic flat stroke with the pressure or ball shape in the center of the stroke and the angle of the chisel at about two o'clock would require the same brush control as an "S" stroke (Fig.13).

Begin by touching the chisel edge of the brush to the surface. Move in the direction of the chisel, applying no pressure. Change direction, continue to pull, applying pressure in the center, release pressure, resume to a chisel and continue to pull. Change direction following the angle of the chisel and create a finished line resembling the beginning of the stroke. Variations on this exercise would include lengthening the beginning and ends and changing the size and thicknesses of the center of the stroke and also, eliminating the beginning and/or end of the stroke (chisel) (Fig. 14). Changing the last two steps, from stop and lift, to "wisping off" produces yet another variation.

"C" OR "U" STROKES

Begin and end on the chisel edge of the brush. Move slowly through its rounded shape, applying pressure to the center of the stroke (Fig. 15). The "ball" or fullest part of this stroke would be in the middle (Fig. 16).

Touch the surface with the chisel edge of the brush. Begin to move along the chisel in a straight line. Change direction of the movement without turning the

Fig. 15. "C" or "U" strokes.

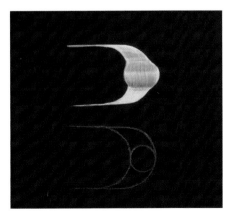

Fig. 16. Motion of the stroke.

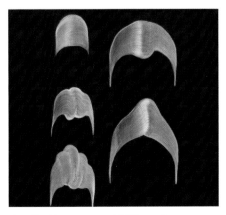

Fig. 17. Variations of "C" stroke.

brush, and without applying added pressure. As you approach the middle, apply greatest pressure in the very center of the stroke. Continue to move, releasing pressure at the same rate previously applied, moving through the curved shape, back onto the chisel edge and finish the stroke. Stop. Lift.

Variations are created, for example, by varying the pressure and shortening the beginning and the ending of the stroke. Leaning on one side or the other will create a different shape within the stroke. Wiggling as pressure is applied will also produce variety (Fig. 17).

"CRESCENT" STROKE

This stroke is very different from the "C" and "U" strokes and also all of the strokes described previously. In order to execute this stroke, you need to vary the angle of the chisel or turn the brush as you move through the steps. In all of the other strokes, once the beginning angle of the brush is determined, the angle remains the same to the end of the stroke (Fig. 18).

Once the spot or destination is marked, point the chisel of the brush to the spot and, in this example, at about ten o'clock. Move in a straight line on the chisel without applying any pressure. Begin to change direction, focusing on a rounded shape. As the brush moves, the chisel edge of the brush continues to point to the destination. As you reach the center of the stroke, the chisel of the brush will be at twelve o'clock. Continue to move in the rounded shape, releasing pressure, until you have reached two o'clock with the brush back on its chisel edge, pointing to the destination.

You can vary this stroke by applying pressure at different points throughout the stroke.

FILLED-IN CIRCLE

Like the crescent stroke, this too requires the turning of the brush. As you turn a

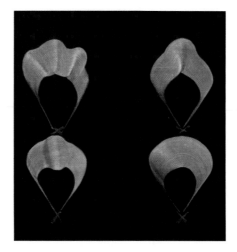
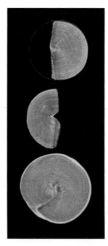

(left) Fig. 18. Crescent with variations. (right) Fig. 19. Filled circle.

brush you must be certain to move slowly to allow the brush hairs time to catch up to each other. Position the brush at twelve o'clock on the chisel edge. The brush should be at 90° to the surface. Lean the brush slightly in the direction of the stroke and begin to move only the outside hairs of the brush, keeping the inside hairs fixed in one spot (which will be the center of the circle.) Doing half of a circle is not too difficult (Fig. 19).

This seems to be just about as far as you can turn the brush, without twisting your arm and body and losing control of the shape.

In order to do a full circle, begin in the same fashion. Position the brush at twelve o'clock so that it feels comfortable between your fingers. Now, roll the brush back between your fingers, forcing the wrist to follow, winding up or coiling your arm/hand. Touch the surface and unwind, keeping the inside of the chisel in one spot and allowing the outside to move around to create the circle. Allow time for the hairs to regroup, rolling the handle back to its starting position and beyond.

LINEWORK

There are many variations and uses for strokework done with a liner. You can achieve a wide variety of useful strokes by pulling it at varying speeds, applying

pressure at different times, using different consistencies of paint, and by changing the angle of the brush.

Liner brushes vary and there is no substitute for a good one. Choose one that allows for several variations of linework without changing brush sizes, and one that will hold a good deal of paint to allow for continuous strokework. Choose a medium length of hair for ease of control (Fig. 20).

To load your liner (acrylic paints) prepare the brush in water. Move the wet brush to your puddle of paint. Lay on its side, and wiggle the wet hairs in the side of the puddle. For most linework you will want to work with an ink-like consistency of paint. If you need to go back and pick up more water, do so with the liner, and move back to the paint puddle.

When you are happy with the even amount of paint in the brush, reshape the pointed tip of the brush before proceeding to your work. Hold the brush upright and touch the tip to your soft absorbent towel, removing any excess water from the brush.

Approach your work with the brush at 90° or at a right angle to the surface. For almost all linework, the brush should be used in an upright position throughout the entire stroke so that the paint flows freely and easily from the tip of the

Fig. 20. Linework strokework.

Fig. 21. "M" and "W" shapes.

Fig. 22. Double-loaded linework with varying pressure.

brush hairs. Use your arms to move the brush, not your fingers or wrist. Do not turn your brush while you are stroking.

Applying pressure changes the stroke. Breaking the stroke up, or moving in curved shapes can also create different strokes.

Paint scrolls by using "m" and "w" shapes with constant pressure or with pressure within the strokes (Fig. 21). Double-loading your liner, or side-loading with one color, will change the look of the line work and in some cases add the appearance of highlighting or shading (Fig. 22).

Enjoy using these basic strokes to paint the porcelain egg strokework design on the following pages.

STROKEWORK FLORAL PATTERN

Strokework Floral

Designed by Heather Redick, CDA

MATERIALS

PALETTE
FolkArt Artist's Pigments:
Titanium White
FolkArt Acrylics:
French Blue

BRUSHES
Robert Simmons Expression:
#4, #6 filbert
¾" flat wash
Heather Redick Brush:
10/0 liner

SURFACE
6½" porcelain egg with 2" stand
   by *Porcelain Tole Treasures* (or
   use any egg of your choice)

OTHER SUPPLIES
See Basic Supplies, page 2
Masterson's Sta-Wet Palette
White transfer paper

SOURCES
See page 127

INSTRUCTIONS

PREPARATION

Select a porcelain, wooden, or even emu egg, of any size, and re-size the pattern to suit. Prepare the surface by sanding and, if necessary, sealing. Refer to pages 5–7 for surface preparation instructions.

Trace the pattern on page 37 onto tracing paper. Transfer the pattern to your egg using white transfer paper (see Transferring the Design, page 7).

PAINTING PROCEDURE

Basecoat with at least two coats of French Blue, using a large ¾" flat wash brush. Sand, if necessary, between coats.

Refer to the strokework instructions at the beginning of this chapter and the worksheet below to fill in the pattern areas with flowers and leaves using the #4 or #6 filbert brush. Pull each stroke separately. Do not go over the strokes.

Using the 10/0 liner brush, add linework to fill the space and give definition to the leaf veins. Also place the dotted flower centers.

FINISHING

Erase any transfer lines. Varnish with your favorite finish.

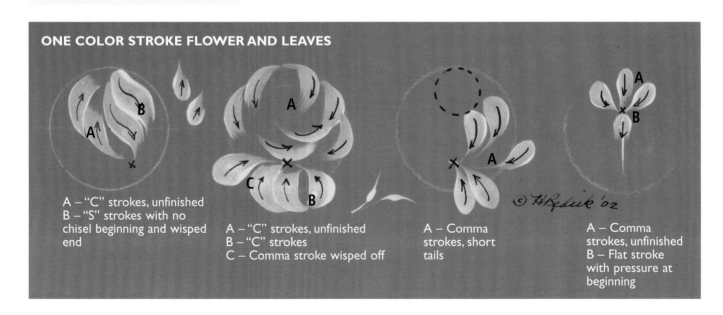

ONE COLOR STROKE FLOWER AND LEAVES

A – "C" strokes, unfinished
B – "S" strokes with no chisel beginning and wisped end

A – "C" strokes, unfinished
B – "C" strokes
C – Comma stroke wisped off

A – Comma strokes, short tails

A – Comma strokes, unfinished
B – Flat stroke with pressure at beginning

About Phillip Myer and Andy Jones

Perhaps synergy explains the volume of creative outpouring and impressive painting credentials of Phillip C. Myer and Andy B. Jones, who team together as PCM Studios in Atlanta, Georgia. Together Phillip and Andy design and create custom-painted furniture, accessories, and interiors, and produce unfinished wood pieces, products, books, brushes, and videos for the decorative painter. They teach seminars on decorative painting and faux finishes at their studios, as well as across the United States and internationally.

Phillip C. Myer earned his Bachelor of Fine Arts degree from the University of the Arts (Philadelphia) and after graduation worked as an editor and art director. A 26-year member of the Society of Decorative Painters, he has numerous books to his credit. He won the National Art Materials Trade Association's Silver Star Print Award and the National Paperbox Packaging Association's Silver Award for Package Design.

Andy B. Jones, with a Bachelor of Arts degree from Florida State University (Tallahassee) previously managed an art gallery. He's been teaching decorative painting for 21 years and has also authored numerous books as well as a video on furniture finishing. He's been a member of the SDP for 19 years, earning the Certified Decorative Artist (CDA) award. Working at PCM Studios the two have collaborated on a variety of books and magazine articles.

Together Phillip and Andy have brought their painting passion to television, appearing on several different networks. How-to videos to their credit include *Marbleizing Technique*, *Wall Glazing Technique*, and *Decorating Techniques*. Three of Phillip's and two of Andy's hand-painted Christmas ornaments are in the collection of the Smithsonian Institution; one of Andy's ornaments is in the White House collection and one of Phillip's is in the Blair House (the White House's guest home) collection. Phillip and Andy have earned a reputation for fabulous faux finishes, and the faux rose marble on this box is a splendid example of this easy technique.

(top) The three boxes were gold-leafed and then a rich Burnt Umber glaze was mottled with a textured pattern using a chamois tool. Rich, wine-colored grapes combine beautifully with the dark background.

(middle) A faux green serpentine marble was painted on the top of this chest. A baroque-style pattern of scrolls, roses, and daisies were added. The piece was then aged with an earth-tone glaze.

(bottom) The desktop and side panels of this elegant desk have a light marbleized finish. The floral design and scrolls were then wrapped around the soft faux marble.

40

Paint and Faux Finishes

By Phillip C. Myer and Andy B. Jones, CDA
of PCM Studios

PAINT AND FAUX FINISHES MAKE IDEAL BACKGROUNDS OR TRIM elements for your decorative painting. A paint finish is simply a random or abstract pattern such as sponging, ragging or texturizing. A paint finish is not meant to duplicate a real surface; it just creates a texture or pattern on a surface. A faux finish is an effect that is meant to duplicate a real surface such as marble, wood, stone, or metal. The French word *faux* means false or fake. Faux finishes are "tricks" that allow you to paint fanciful textures or duplicate the look of exotic wood, fabric, marble, or stone.

By combining faux or paint finishes with your decorative painting you can create works of art with a special flair. Adding subtle interest to the background or a more dynamic look to a trim element, the use of finishes makes a great addition to your decorative painting repertoire. Remember that as you plan your project, either the decorative painting or the faux finish has to be the star of the show. They cannot compete for attention. As a rule of thumb, let the decorative painting take center stage and let the paint or faux finish be a supporting element.

We hope you enjoy creating the simple paint and faux finishes on the following pages as well as the elegant box project showing a combination of painted finishes and decorative painting. The box was given a subtle stippled finish using metallic colors to give a rich look. The marbleized accents repeat the pink tones used to paint the rose. The rose has a warm tone to it which is echoed in the warm tones of the marble. It is important that all elements relate to each other.

SIMPLE PAINT FINISHES

There is no limit to the variety of looks you can create by combining painted finishes with decorative painting. The examples pictured on this page range from country to formal. You can decide how elaborate you want your piece. Sometimes a very simple finish will show off the painting to its best advantage. Other pieces will require more elaborate finishes.

There are numerous books available with instructions for a variety of paint and faux finishes. We give you instructions for just a tiny sampling of the many effects you can achieve. We hope that these will inspire you to include faux finishes in your decorative painting.

Chamois Texture Finish

FolkArt Acrylics: Tapioca, Heartland Blue

Brushes: Faux finish brushes by *Silver Brush: Series 9095S* basecoat, *Series 9093S* glaze/varnish, chamois tool by *Plaid*

Miscellaneous Items: *FolkArt Acrylic Spray Sealer, FolkArt Glazing Medium*

Instructions

Basecoat the desired surface with several coats of Tapioca, using a basecoat brush. Apply enough coats to achieve opaque coverage. Let dry thor-

oughly, then spray with sealer.

Create a desired glaze color. We used Heartland Blue, a soft country blue, for the sample (right). Then add glazing medium to the acrylic paint in about a 1:1 ratio. Brush the blue glaze color on the surface using a glaze application brush.

Pick up a chamois tool or crumple chamois fabric and hit the surface to impart a textured pattern. Dab and hit the surface randomly so you do not repeat a pattern across the surface. Continue this process until you have developed a textured pattern across the entire surface.

Mahogany Woodgrain Finish

FolkArt Acrylics: Light Red Oxide, Burnt Umber, Burnt Sienna, and Pure Black

Brushes: Faux finish brushes by *Silver Brush: Series 9095S* basecoat, *Series 9093S* 1" glaze/varnish, *Series 9091S* 2" blending, *Series 9098S* 1½" flogger, *Series 9090* ¾" mop, *Series 2504S* fan

Miscellaneous items: *FolkArt Acrylic Spray Sealer, FolkArt Glazing Medium*

Instructions

Basecoat the desired surface with several coats of Light Red Oxide using a basecoat brush. Apply ample coats for opaque coverage. Let dry thoroughly, then spray with sealer.

(top) A verdigris finish on copper panels creates a striking backdrop for this rooster.
(second from top) A grouping of roses, lilacs, and leaves adorn a camel-back trunk. A band of gold leaf trims the trunk out.
(bottom, left) Yellow and purple irises are set against a graduated background of a dull green tone. Trim on this cabinet features a faux green marble finish.
(bottom, right) This chest of drawers was sponge-painted with many layers of creams and pink tones before the floral groupings were added.

CHAMOIS TEXTURE FINISH

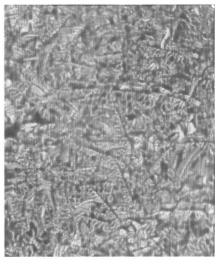

Brush on glaze randomly.

Hit glaze with chamois tool or cloth.

Continue creating texture with chamois.

MAHOGANY WOODGRAIN FINISH

Apply random patches of BS, BU, BLK.

Blend colors with blending softener.

Hit wet glaze with flogger brush.

Apply heart of grain pattern in arc with fan brush.

Continue adding arching grain marks and blend.

For straight grain, run fan brush across the surface.

Create three glaze mixtures adding equal parts of glazing medium to the following individual colors: Burnt Sienna, Burnt Umber, Pure Black.

Pick up a glaze application brush and place random color patches of Burnt Sienna, Burnt Umber, and smaller patches of Pure Black on the surface. Blend the color patches together using a 2" blending softener brush. Break up the patches but do not over-blend (creating one brown color).

Hit the surface with a flogger brush in a hop and hit motion to impart a fine grain-like pattern. Allow the flogging to thoroughly dry.

Next, over-graining can be added to the surface. This can be executed in a heart of the wood grain pattern or a straight grain pattern. Load a fan brush with the black glaze then tap off excess paint from the brush on your palette. For a heart of the wood grain pattern, drag the fan brush in an arching pattern from the bottom upward. After you place an arch of black markings, lightly blend downward over them with the mop brush. Continue making a series of upside down "U" arches around the surface, blending them with the mop brush.

For a straight grain pattern, load the fan brush with the black glaze, tap the fan brush on the palette and stroke across the surface in a somewhat straight line. Blend these markings as you go using the mop brush.

CHAMPAGNE AND ROSES

The "Champagne and Roses" project on pages 46–49 makes use of both a paint and a faux finish. Follow the instructions below to complete the special finish areas of the project.

Stippled Finish

FolkArt Acrylics: Tapioca, Silver Sterling, and Asphaltum
Brushes: Faux finish brushes by *Silver Brush: Series 9095S* basecoat, *Series 9093S glaze/varnish,* stippler by *Plaid*
Miscellaneous items: *FolkArt Acrylic Spray Sealer, FolkArt Glazing Medium*

Instructions

Basecoat the desired surface with several coats of Tapioca using a basecoat brush. Apply ample coats for an opaque coverage. Let dry thoroughly, then spray with sealer.

Create a desired glaze color. Here mixing 2 parts Silver Sterling to 1 part Asphaltum created a champagne color. Then add glazing medium to the acrylic paint in about a 50/50 ratio. Brush the champagne glaze color on the surface using a glaze application brush.

Pick up the stippler brush and hit the surface in an up and down bouncing motion. This will immediately begin to even out the glaze, remove brush marks, and impart a fine dot-like pattern to the surface. Complete the entire surface in this manner. Allow to dry.

For a more shaded look, load a dry stippler brush with additional glaze on the corner of the brush. Place this additional color on the surface at the edges and in corners. Bounce color out into the existing dry stippled pattern so you do not see where the color stops. This should give a pleasing graduated look.

Pink Marble Finish

FolkArt Acrylics: Potpourri Rose, True Burgundy, Portrait, Titanium White, Burnt Umber
Brushes: Faux finish brushes by *Silver Brush: Series 9095S* basecoat, *Series 9093S* glaze/varnish, *Series 9094S* 2" Blending, *Series 9090S* ¾" mop
Miscellaneous Items: Marbleizing feather, sea sponge, *FolkArt Acrylic Spray Sealer, FolkArt Glazing Medium*

Instructions

Basecoat the desired surface with several coats of Potpourri Rose using a basecoat brush. Apply ample coats to achieve opaque coverage. Let dry thoroughly, then spray with sealer.

Next create three values of pink glaze mixtures: a dark pink of 50% True Burgundy + 30% Burnt Umber + 20% Potpourri Rose, a medium pink of 80% Rose Potpourri + 20% True Burgundy, and a light pink of 80% Portrait + 20% True Burgundy. Add equal parts glazing medium to these pink mixtures.

Load a sea sponge with medium value pink mixture and dab diagonally on the surface. Next to these color dabs add dark value pink mixture. Then randomly add smaller patches of the light pink mixture. Pick up a 2" blending softener brush and blend these color patches to remove distinct sponge marks. The markings from the sponge should become blurred.

To add veins to the marble, add equal parts glazing medium to Titanium White + a small amount of water. Load a feather at the tip, extending about one inch from the tip. Loosely hold the feather in your hand and stroke through the wet pink colors. Place the veins in a diagonal direction for a pleasing flow to the line. Allow the feather to deposit thin and thick areas to the vein structure. Place larger "primary" veins on the surface and then add "secondary" smaller veins using just the tip of the feather. The veins will look more natural if you carry them off the surface or let them connect to another vein structure.

Soften veins with a mop brush. Stroke over the veins in the same direction as the way the veins are flowing across the surface. If you blend across the veins, they will appear smeared and not softened.

STIPPLED FINISH

Brush on glaze randomly.

Hit glaze with stippler brush.

Once dry, darken corners/edges.

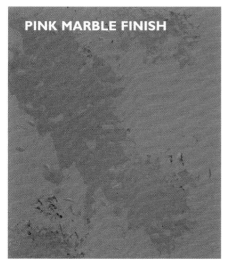

PINK MARBLE FINISH

Hit surface with sponge + medium pink.

Load sponge with dark pink + dab.

Add smaller areas of light pink with sponge.

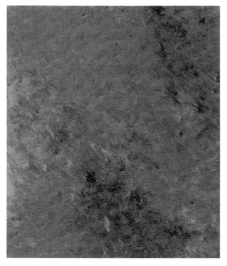

Soften/blend sponge marks with blending softener brush.

Add primary veins with feather and blend with mop brush.

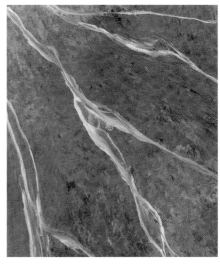

Add secondary/smaller veins and blend with mop brush.

45

Champagne and Roses

Designed by Phillip C. Myer and Andy B. Jones, CDA

MATERIALS

PALETTE

FolkArt Artist's Pigments:
Burnt Umber
Dioxazine Purple
Hauser Green Medium
Ice Blue
Olive Green Dark
Portrait
Titanium White
True Burgundy
Warm White
Yellow Light
FolkArt Acrylics:
Potpourri Rose
Tapioca

BRUSHES

Silver Brush Ltd.:
#4, #8 flat shaders: *Golden Natural™ Series 2002S*
#2 script liner: *Golden Natural™ Series 2007S*
#6, #8 filberts: *Ruby Satin™ Series 2053S*
1" varnish brush: *Series 9093S*
See page 44 for faux finish brushes

SURFACE

Mini Bombay box 9" x 11" x 3½" by *Valhalla Designs*

OTHER SUPPLIES

See Basic Supplies, page 2
White pigmented stain-blocking primer
Painter's tape
FolkArt Acrylic Spray Sealer
FolkArt Water Base Varnish/Satin

SOURCES

See page 127

INSTRUCTIONS

PREPARATION

Basecoat the raw wood box with a stain-blocking primer. Allow to dry then sand with medium- and fine-grade sandpaper. Remove sanding dust with a tack rag. Basecoat the top of the box with Tapioca and the bottom with Potpourri Rose. Apply several coats until opaque. Seal the basecoats with several light mistings of *Acrylic Spray Sealer*.

Create the stippled finish over the entire top of the box and on the ball feet. Let that finish dry and mark off a 1" band about ¾" in from the edge. Mask off the 1" band with tape. Create the pink marble finish on the bottom of the box and in this 1" banded area. Let finishes dry.

Trace and transfer the rose pattern on page 48 using white transfer paper (see Transferring the Design, page 7).

PAINTING THE DESIGN
Leaves

Begin mixing a dull green by adding a small amount of Burnt Umber to Hauser Green Medium and mixing with a palette knife. Using the #8 flat brush, undercoat the leaves with this mixture. Allow the first coat to dry and then apply a second coat to achieve an opaque coverage. Allow to dry.

Sideload the #8 flat brush with Olive Green Dark. Apply the shading color where one leaf goes under another or under the rose (see shading detail on page 48). Use this shading to establish the center vein area. Let dry. Repeat this step to intensify the shading on the leaves.

Begin highlighting the leaves with the #8 filbert brush. Load the brush with a scant amount of the undercoat green. First establish the center vein area by highlighting on the light side of the vein and on the opposite outside edge of the leaf. Use this color to soften the line where the shading ends. Add a small amount of Yellow Light to the undercoat mix and apply another layer of highlighting in the same manner as described before. Remember that as you highlight, each layer of color will be lighter than the previous layer and will take up less space. This will allow the eye to "blend" the colors, thus creating a gradation of value. Add more yellow to the mix and continue highlighting. Now, add a small amount of Warm White to the highlight mix. Apply the highlight in the same manner. You may want to add a little more Warm White to the mixture and apply a final highlight to the leaves.

Add some tints and accents. To apply them, sideload the #8 flat brush with True Burgundy + a little Burnt Umber and apply the accents near the base of the leaf. Start on the edge and gently work the color into the leaf. Paint the tints with Potpourri Rose and apply in the lighter area of the leaf.

Add the leaf veins using the #2 script liner brush and a light green made from Hauser Green Medium + Yellow Light + Warm White. Apply the center vein first and then paint the radiating veins.

Rose

Undercoat the rose with Potpourri Rose, first using the script liner brush to

outline it, then filling in using the #8 flat brush. Apply a second coat to ensure an opaque surface on which to work.

Transfer the petals to the rose using gray transfer paper. Be sure you transfer the design accurately. It is very difficult to paint a rose if you cannot follow the design easily. Mix a little Burnt Umber into True Burgundy to make a deep burgundy color. Sideload the #4 flat brush with the mixture and begin to apply the shading to the rose. Shade where a petal rolls or flips over, where one petal goes behind another petal (refer to worksheet and shading detail for placement).

The highlighting begins with the #6 filbert loaded with a scant amount of Potpourri Rose. Use this to soften the shading and establish the positions of the highlights. Place the highlights on the center of a petal's flips and where the bowl of the rose bulges. Be sure that the highlight follows the contour of the flip. If you allow the shape of the highlight to vary from the petal shape, the rose will appear misshapen. Add a layer of highlights to the rose using the same technique, but this time use Portrait.

Add some Warm White to the Portrait and add a fourth layer of highlights to the rose. You may want to add a little Titanium White to the mixture to establish the brightest highlights.

To complete the rolls and flips of the rose, you need to add reflected light to the lower edge of the turns. Mix Ice Blue + Dioxazine Purple and load the script liner brush with the mixture. Apply thin lines of varying widths to the lower edges of the petals. Add more Ice Blue to the mixture and add a few brighter accents to some of the larger petals.

If desired, load the liner brush with the dark burgundy color and intensify the shadows under the flips. This will add more dimension to the rose. You may accent the rose with a little Yellow Light, thinned until it's transparent and

sideloaded on the #4 flat brush. Add these accents *very* sparingly and then only to a few petals. Study the finished painting for placement.

Paint the rose's calyxes using the same colors as used for the leaves.

FINISHING

Optional Step: Using a ruling pen, add a fine dark pink (50% True Burgundy + 30% Burnt Umber + 20% Potpourri Rose) pinstripe around the pink marble banded area and ¼" from the edge of the box top.

After all the paint/faux finishes and decorative painting is complete, protect the painting with several coats of a water-based varnish.

Shading Detail

CHAMPAGNE AND ROSES PATTERN

48

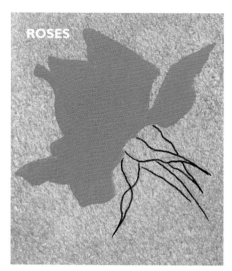

Undercoat the rose using Potpourri Rose.

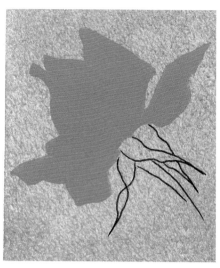

Transfer the petals to the rose with gray transfer paper.

Shade the rose petals with True Burgundy + Burnt Umber.

Begin highlighting.

Continue highlighting.

Add reflected light and additional shadows.

LEAVES

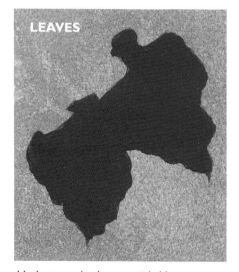

Undercoat the leaves with Hauser Green Medium + Burnt Umber.

Shade the leaves with Olive Green Dark.

Add secondary/smaller veins and blend with mop brush.

About Donna Dewberry

Mother of seven and grandmother to an ever-expanding extended family, Donna Dewberry taught herself to paint in the quiet evening hours, relaxing after a busy day of carpooling, cooking, and storytelling, Donna would pull out her paints and learn directly through trial and error. Little did she know that her "baby steps" in decorative painting would eventually lead to her own recognizable style, an original stroke technique, and a career that would blossom into a thriving business of international renown.

Donna is best known as the creator of the FolkArt "One-Stroke" technique of Plaid Enterprises. From these easy strokes flow garlands and bouquets of luscious flowers and greenery in her signature breezy, casual style. She developed a "One-Stroke" Certification Program for teachers to instruct her technique, and has certified over 2,000 students. As a demonstrator and teacher Donna has taught thousands of students around the world. She's painted over 1,200 homes as an interior designer.

Donna and her husband, Marc, have written over 38 instructional books, nine self-teaching videos, reusable teaching guides, and have a line of specialty brushes and supplies. You may even have seen Donna on television, perhaps on HGTV's *Our Place* and *Home Matters*; PBS's *Paint, Paint, Paint, One-Stroke Painting with Donna Dewberry,* and *Our Home*; and QVC Shopping Channel. Donna's on-line magazine, *The Stroking Edge (www.thestrokingedge.com)*, debuted in 2000. Her columns appear in six separate magazines, and she has published over 200 articles for home, decorating, and craft issues. Her gift line of products sell in retail stores and catalogues worldwide. Other recent ventures include Donna Dewberry designs for wallpaper, Farberware dishware, Spring's baby fabric and Westpoint Stevens bedding.

Best known for her floral designs for furniture and home decor, Donna Dewberry has taught her method to countless numbers of painters through her classes, books, and television appearances.

One-Stroke Painting

By Donna Dewberry

I BEGAN PAINTING MANY YEARS AGO. I HAD ALWAYS LOVED BEAUTIFUL painting, and wanted to decorate my home for my young, growing family. I truly admired beautiful ceramic painting with its layers of basecoating, blending, shading, and highlighting, but there was no time for classes. I was lucky to steal away a little time at night for painting!

Learning at home on my own seemed to be the best option. When I studied painted items, it seemed they were painted with more than one color on the brush. Making use of my past experience with cake-decorating classes, I decided to apply the same principles for layering and building to my painted roses and other flowers. I started at the back and worked my way forward. It was only later that I learned my method was very different from traditional tole painting.

The main difference between the One-Stroke technique of double loading and traditional double loading is that the traditional method is used along with blended and built-up strokework. The One-Stroke technique uses two or more colors to achieve shading, blending, and highlighting in each stroke. So a full leaf, for example, would only use two strokes, one for each leaf half, with each stroke being complete. There is actually a One-Stroke leaf that can be completed with only one stroke! This method really came in handy when I later got a contract to paint tinware. If you try to go back and blend on tinware, sometimes the paint just lifts right off the surface. The One-Stroke method worked perfectly, and the tinware pieces could be completed in a short period of time.

Another difference between the methods is that the One-Stroke technique is a freehand method. Patterns are not necessary, which saves transferring time. However, people who are new to One-Stroke techniques generally choose to use my patterns as a guide for placement. The main focus is to create something beautiful in a quick and easy fashion.

ONE-STROKE METHOD

Traditional multi-loading with more than two colors is usually done with a round brush that is fully loaded with one color, then pulled through several other colors (with the direction of the stroke giving the different shading). Multi-loading in One-Stroke offers the benefits of dramatic shading and variety in our work. When painting leaves, I might pick up white for the center one time, then using the same brush, I pick up a soft yellow or beige for another leaf to create variety.

It is important to remember that when double loading your brush, be sure to load enough paint. Traditional tole painting uses much less paint on the brush. A big problem with beginning One-Stroke painters is not using enough paint. A second problem is not pushing hard enough. You must push the bristles because that is part of what creates the beautiful blending.

I highly recommend the use of *FolkArt* paint with this technique because of its thick and creamy consistency, similar to tube paint. This is especially helpful with the blending. Most projects can be painted with fewer than ten colors. They are favorite colors that I enjoy using in most of my paintings.

Floating medium is the "fluff" that the paint is made from. It is clear and allows your paint to be applied more smoothly on dryer surfaces like paper or a wall. When using floating medium, place a puddle on your palette and after fully loading your brush, dip the tip of your brush into the puddle. Then work into your brush by stroking once or twice in the area where you loaded your brush. Do not use too much floating medium or your project will be over-blended and the colors muddy.

BRUSH TECHNIQUES

The use of One-Stroke brushes that I've developed is essential to achieving success with the One-Stroke technique. They have been designed especially for this type of strokework. A basic set contains the #12, ¾", and the #2 script liner. This set, along with the regular scruffy brush (four brushes total) allow you to paint most of the projects I have created. Additional brushes allow you to make the designs smaller or larger.

To follow is an explanation for the use and/or purpose of each brush. Understanding this will help you in completing the tavern sign project on page 56.

Flat Brush Technique

I find it's easiest for me to achieve the shading I want using a flat brush. One-Stroke flat brushes are different from most flats in that the bristles are longer with less thickness in the body of the brush, and with a thinner ferrule. This allows more paint to be loaded onto the bristles so there will be enough paint to complete the whole stroke. The chisel edge at the tip is used to paint stems, vines, etc. without having to change brushes—another time-saver.

A traditional decorative painting flat brush would lose the chisel edge with as much paint as we use with this technique. As you will see, a sharp chisel edge, or tip of the bristles, is essential to the technique since most of the strokes begin and end on the chisel edge of the brush (our stems and other lines are drawn with it). Do not let paint dry in the ferrule because you will lose your chisel edge.

One-Stroke flats are available in eight sizes: #2, #6, #8, #10, #12, #16, ¾", 1", and 1½". Keep in mind when choosing a brush that everyone's comfort zone varies, and as one painter is comfortable using a size #12, another painter may be just as comfortable with size ¾". With this in mind, use the size brush with which you feel most comfortable, within the scale of the design. The stroke is best when the bristles are being pushed down sufficiently. It is best to use the largest size that is comfortable to you for your design.

The first time you use the brush, you should remove the sizing from the bristles. Clean in the brush basin, using the grid at the bottom, brushing back and forth several times. Dry with a paper towel before using. For future painting sessions just dampen the bristles in water and dry by laying them gently on a paper towel on one side, then turning and repeating on the other. When cleaning these brushes, you may rake them gently in the bottom of the brush basin, as the bristles are not natural and therefore do not have as much of a tendency to break as natural bristles.

Loading the flat brush. Refer to photos (opposite and on page 54). Squeeze the paint out onto a foam plate into about 1" puddles. After dampening the flat brush and wiping it on a paper towel, dip one corner into a puddle of paint, then turn the brush over and dip the other corner into the second color. (For example, use green and white when painting leaves.) The colors should form triangles on the brush and meet in the middle. Then fully load the brush by stroking it back and forth on the palette; the key to loading the brush is pushing really hard.

After several strokes, pick up more paint and repeat. Do this until the colors meet in the center and paint fills the brush two-thirds of the way up the bristles. Now that your brush is loaded, pick up paint on each corner to begin painting. Don't stroke the brush anymore on the palette. As you continue to work, load the paint only on the corners of the brush after each stroke, or as needed. After you have been working for awhile, the brush may begin to feel dry or your bristles may begin to separate. If this happens, it is time to work more paint into the bristles as you did when first

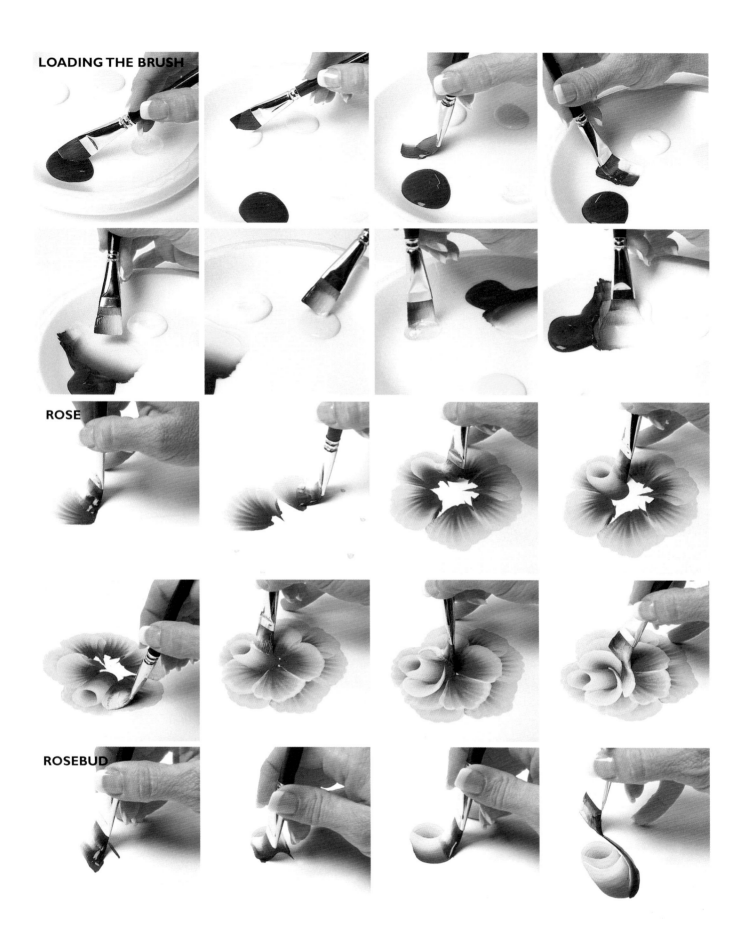

LOADING THE BRUSH

ROSE

ROSEBUD

53

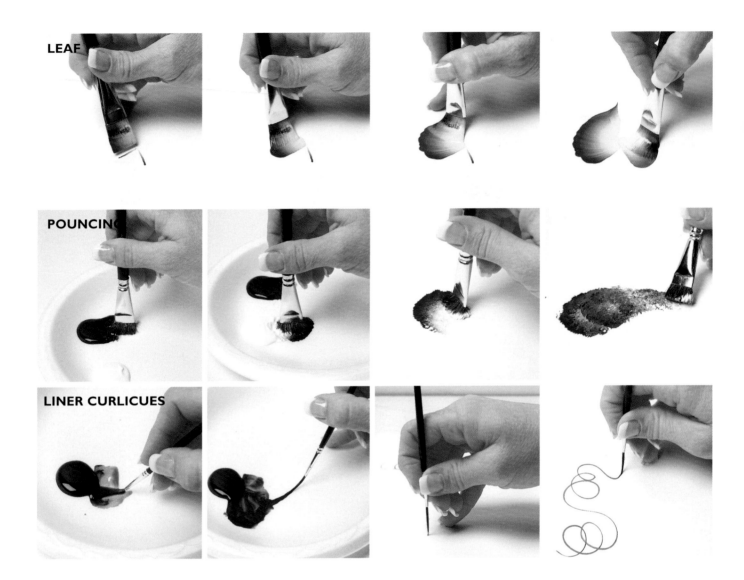

LEAF

POUNCING

LINER CURLICUES

loading the brush. As we paint it should feel like spreading soft butter. If it is not that smooth, it's time to reload. Always remember to make sure you have enough paint on the brush!

To multi-load the brush with more than two colors, first fully load the brush with the two basic colors (such as green and white). Then pick up light colors on the lighter side of the brush (such as yellow on the white side). If you have darker colors to add they would go on the dark side (like brown on the green side). As you paint, reload your brush by picking up both colors on each corner. Do not re-blend the colors.

Double loading a mini brush is a little different than loading the larger brushes. Dip the entire bristle section of the brush into the darker paint puddle. Pull the brush out of the puddle to smooth the paint into the bristles. Pull on the edge of the brush along the edge of the lighter paint puddle. After each stroke, pull along the lighter color to pick up more paint. Go back to the darker paint and reload as the brush gets dry.

Scruffy Brush Technique

Before using the scruffy you need to "fluff the scruff." While holding the brush, form the natural bristles into a fan

shape by gently pulling on them, fluffing out from the center to spread. Then, with the brush bristles in the palm of your hand and the brush handle perpendicular to your palm; twist the bristles until you have shaped the brush into a fan shape. Now you are ready to pounce into paint and begin. Don't worry if you lose a few hairs the first time in use.

When fluffed, the scruffy brush is used for painting mosses, wisteria, lilacs, certain hair and fur, faux finishing, and shading textures. This brush is not used with water. When cleaning the brush, pounce the bristles in the brush basin rather than raking them so you will not break the natural bristles. When painting with a new color, dry the brush thoroughly by squeezing it gently with a paper towel, paying special attention to removing all excess water from the ferrule. Then "fluff the scruff" again to prepare to paint. This is also the best way to prepare your brush for storing.

Loading the scruffy brush. After "fluffing the scruff," load the brush by pouncing one side into the edge of the first puddle of color (refer to photo on opposite page). Then pounce the other half of the scruffy brush into the edge of the second puddle of color. Imagine the brush divided in half. The two colors should always be separate on the brush when reloading. Do not pounce on your palette. This will cause your paint to be over-blended. You should be able to see both colors plus a blend on your project. A single blended color indicates over-blending. To prevent this, pick up more paint.

The scruffy brush can be multi-loaded in the same way as other brushes, pouncing into light colors on one side and dark colors on the other side. This creates very pretty moss when several colors are used.

Script Liner Technique

Use the #1 liner (script mini) for small detail work where a lot of control is needed. Use the #2 script liner where less control is needed such as curlicues and string ribbons.

Loading the script liner. This is one time that water is needed for the technique. Wet the liner, then load as follows: Prepare an inky paint mixture by loading paint onto your palette and dipping the brush into water. With the brush lying on the surface, roll the brush along the side of the paint puddle and pull out a small puddle of paint (refer to photos on opposite page). Repeat two or three more times, adding

(top)Painting a mailbox is quick and easy using a flat brush for the leaves, a scruffy for the wisteria, and a liner for the tendrils.
(bottom) Painting fruit is as easy as flowers, using the same techniques and brushes.

more water until inky. Roll into the diluted paint to load it, twirling the brush, and pull it out to the side of the palette. Do this until the brush is well loaded. Use the tip of the brush when painting.

These brushes can be cleaned like the flat brushes. Be gentle but clean thoroughly.

Left-Handed Painters

• Always start where I say to end and end your stroke where I indicate to start.

• When you are stroking leaves, turn your practice sheets, or worksheets, so you stroke the tip of the leaf towards your body.

Roses and Violets

Designed by Donna Dewberry

INSTRUCTIONS

PREPARATION

Lightly sand the wooden sign surface. Basecoat with two coats of Wicker White, sanding lightly between coats. Let dry. If desired, trace the pattern on page 58 on tracing paper and transfer to the sign (see Transferring the Design, page 7).

LETTERING

Load the #6 flat with Thicket. Paint any lettering or numbering that you would like for personalizing your sign. Using a bit of floating medium will help the paint to flow more smoothly.

MATERIALS

PALETTE

FolkArt Acrylics:
Berry Wine
Purple Passion
Sunflower
Thicket
Wicker White

BRUSHES

FolkArt One-Stroke Brushes:
#6, #8, #10, #12, ¾" flat
#2 script liner

SURFACE

Wood tavern sign, 8½" x 10¾" by
  Oakcreek Woodworks

OTHER SUPPLIES

See Basic Supplies, page 2
FolkArt Floating Medium
FolkArt Acrylic Clearcoate Matte
  Sealer

SOURCES

See page 127

PROCEDURE

Rose

Petals. Double load the ¾" flat with Berry Wine and Wicker White; work colors into the brush to create a soft pink.

With the white to the outer edge, paint five to six shell-like petals to form the outer skirt of the rose. Paint these petals by pushing on the bristles; while pivoting on the Wicker White side, wiggle the bristles to create a shell-like petal. Be sure to overlap each petal. Refer to color worksheet on page 59.

Rosebud (center of rose). Starting on side of rose bud, paint the second row of shell-like petals. Re-stroke the rose bud to clean up strokes. On the chisel edge, starting on the sides of the rosebud, paint center strokes (see worksheet).

Using the same brush, paint the individual rosebuds.

Leaves

Double load the ¾" flat with Thicket and Wicker White, occasionally adding a touch of Berry Wine on the white side. Blend colors to create a soft, muted look. On the chisel edge, leading with Wicker White, paint the rosebud calyx.

Using the same brush, with Thicket to the outer edge, paint big wiggle leaves by pushing, wiggling, and sliding to the tip.

Small Leaves

Double load the #12 flat with Thicket and Wicker White. Occasionally pick up a little Berry Wine or Sunflower on the white side. With thicket to the outer edge, push, then turn and slide back to the chisel edge to paint one-stroke leaves.

Floated (Background) Leaves

Double load the #12 brush with floating medium and a touch of Berry Wine. Work this paint into the floating medium and make a puddle of a soft pink tint. Clean the brush. Use this puddle to load your brush, then paint one-stroke leaves.

Violets

Double load the #8 flat with Purple Passion and Wicker White. With purple to the outer edge, paint five-petal flowers one petal at a time working around the center. On some of the flowers, turn the brush so the white is on the outer edge. Dot the centers with Sunflower. Refer to color worksheet.

Butterflies

Using the same brush and paints, start on the chisel edge at the top of the wings, push and then slide back to the tip. Add the second wing. On the chisel edge, pull in the bottom wings. Refer to color worksheet.

Load the #2 script liner with inky Thicket to paint the body and antennae.

Curlicue Tendrils

Using the same brush and a light touch, paint the curlicue tendrils.

FINISHING

Allow to dry, then finish with two or three coats of *FolkArt Acrylic Clearcoate Matte Sealer.*

ROSE AND VIOLETS
PATTERN
(blue lines
indicate curlicues)

BACKGROUND LEAVES

#12 flat Berry Wine and Floating Medium.

LEAVES

¾" flat Thicket/ Wicker White, touch of Berry Wine.

Push, wiggle, then slide to tip.

Start.

End.

BUTTERFLY

Start.

Slide.

#2 script liner Inky Thicket body and antennae.

Touch and pull.

CALYX

¾" flat Thicket/ Wicker White, chisel edge around rose-buds leading with Wicker White.

For stem, touch, pull down.

On chisel, push and pull.

TENDRILS

#2 script liner with inky Thicket.

SMALL LEAVES

#12 flat Thicket/ Wicker White with Sunflower.

Start.

End.

Pull stem halfway into leaf.

VIOLETS

#10 flat Purple Passion/ Wicker White.

Overlap strokes.

Dot center Sunflower.

ROSEBUDS

¾" flat Berry Wine/ Wicker White.

Start.

End.

Add second layer for bud.

ROSES

Outer skirt; fill in with overlapping petals.

1st

2nd

3rd

4th

5th

Start.

End.

Start chisel strokes from lines.

Start second layer of petals from these lines.

1st

2nd

3rd

1st

2nd

3rd

4th

About Gayle Oram

It took moving to an Alaska fishing village to awaken Gayle Oram's love for rosemaling. Originally settled by Norwegians, the coastal town of Petersburg displays its heritage with quaint touches such as rosemaling painted on the store fronts and shutters. This sparked Gayle's interest as she sought to learn more of this aesthetic. Gayle ponders "Unlike most rosemalers, I cannot find Norwegian roots in my ancestry, unless it goes back to the Viking days when they plundered my Scottish, English, and French ancestors. It must be so because I have such a strong love for the painting and a warm feeling when I visit Norway." Five trips to Norway to seek out and further her study of rosemaling strengthened her love for this style.

Gayle first began painting during her college years while minoring in art, but her first exposure to decorative painting was indirectly through Jo Sonja Jansen. Through numerous influences she came to enjoy all forms of decorative painting. "Building something from raw wood to the finished product is especially gratifying. I love my work and wish there were more hours in the day to get to all those wonderful things waiting for me to decorate."

Gayle has owned her own business since 1982, working at her studio/shop developing a line of clocks and other products for rosemalers and decorative painters. She became a member of the Society of Decorative painters in 1977 and received her Master of Decorative Arts Certification in 1980. One of Gayle's biggest career highlights was receiving her Vesterheim Gold Medal from Vesterheim Norwegian-American Museum in 2000. She has written numerous books and magazine articles and teaches decorative painting around the world, including Japan, where there's much interest in rosemaling. She declares "I truly enjoy sharing decorative painting wherever I am."

Many of Gayle Oram's designs reflect the grace and beauty of classic Norwegian Rosemaling. Shown are designs in the Telemark style (top and right) and Shell rococo style (above).

Norwegian Rosemaling

By Gayle Oram, MDA, VGM

ROSEMALING EMERGED AT DIFFERENT TIMES THROUGHOUT RURAL southern Norway. It was after Christianity arrived and at the time when people learned how to use a chimney and a stove in the corner of the house. Previously, a fire in the center of the house, and a hole in the top of the roof caused houses to be smoky and dirty. With the use of the fireplace and a chimney, houses became much cleaner. People wanted to brighten up their homes by washing the walls and maybe whitewashing. Conditions were ripe for the emergence of decoration to liven up the home. Church and town painters were influenced by the current styles of Europe and some traveled to other countries, bringing back ideas and techniques, then incorporating them into their work. In return, they influenced the country painters, who used their imagination to develop unique design ideas of color and style into a rural folk art.

While studying rosemaling from the past, we note that there are many variations within styles. Each painter exhibited his own characteristic methods, motifs and details. Areas were remote and travel at a minimum in the 18th and 19th Centuries, which was one of the main reasons styles developed differently from valley to valley. There were schools where skilled rosemalers taught others; therefore the student's work resembled that of the teacher's. Some took on characteristics of their teachers; others developed and created in their own way, just as it's happening today. Those who traveled often picked up ideas from others and started incorporating them. In the early 1800s there were so many painters in some areas, that a number left home seeking work elsewhere, some migrating to America.

In the Telemark area, rosemaling as well as music, dance, woodcarving and weaving, developed to a higher level than in most other areas. Perhaps this is because it was so remote and travel so difficult in these mountain communities. Rosemaling can be traced to around 1712 and Thomas Blix, who was an urban painter commissioned to paint churches and other objects in the area. Later in the 1760s, the Telemark style, as we know it, developed from rococo shells and "C-shapes." These gradually changed into plant ornamentation with a basic "C" scroll, or stem, and asymmetrical "S" shapes, sometimes intertwining into beautiful, graceful, flowing designs. Beautiful, creative, and imaginative flower forms of all sizes were tucked among the scrolls, flowing gracefully from the root of the design. Graceful lines and teardrops completed the designs, so that as time went on the rococo feeling was lost.

In each area of rural southern Norway we can see rosemaling developing and changing so that each district, or even valley, developed a distinctive style. Hallingdal was another prolific area. By the early 1800s, there were so many painters that some were forced to leave home to find work in other areas, especially western Norway; some immigrated to America. Herbrand Sata (1753-1830) was an outstanding painter who mastered the rococo style. This gradually developed into his own symmetrical creations with stylized flowers being the dominant feature of his designs. His two sons, Nils Baera (1785-1873) and Embrik Baera (1788-1876) continued in their father's footsteps, creating the basis of the popular Hallingdal style.

It's interesting that in all the folk arts of the world, we can see basic strokes used in different ways to create interesting designs that have lasted and inspired many for hundreds of years. I hope this little bit of history will whet your appetite to want to learn more about rosemaling. Excellent rosemaling reference materials are available through the Vesterheim Norwegian-American Museum, a non-profit organization in Decorah, Iowa devoted to the preservation of this classic art form.

My Os tray design on page 65 is

reflective of a style from the Os region of Norway, in the Hordaland area just south of Bergen. I based this design on the work of Annanias M. Tveit. Johannes Johannessen Tveiteras (1763-1842) is perhaps the first rosemaler from this area. One of his two sons, Nil Tveiteras Midhus (1795-1875) moved to Os in 1820 where he developed his distinctively different style. He combined Telemark

elements with geometric designs and old Hordaland motifs. White, blue or red backgrounds with bright design colors were typical. His son, Annanias Midthus Tveit (1847-1924) further developed the tradition with great creativity and love of color. Rosemaling bloomed late in this area and didn't reach its peak until the turn of the 20th Century.

Scrolls and flowers on the rim of this plate (right) enhance the landscape painted in the Numdedal style of Nore Stovebirke.
Sampler tray (below) displays the lesser known styles of rosemaling.
Worksheet (opposite) shows some basic rosemaling strokes and detailing.

Rosemaling Strokes

Scrolls may be painted in either direction

Root of design

Oval

Double oval

Blended oval

Igloos

¾ round

Round

"S" strokes

Tulip

With light teardrops

Paint light over-strokes while red is wet

Leaf shapes

Details

1. Start with center motif. Paint color by color as numbered.
2. Paint flowers with strokes as numbered.
3. Add detail.
4. Add stems and fill-in detail.

63

Os Tray

Designed by Gayle Oram, MDA, VGM

MATERIALS

PALETTE

Jo Sonja Artist Colors:
Brown Earth
Brown Madder
Burnt Umber
Green Oxide
Raw Sienna
Red Earth
Smoked Pearl (background)
Storm Blue
Teal Green
Warm White
Yellow Oxide

BRUSHES

Loew-Cornell Golden Taklon or Jo Sonja's Sure Touch Golden Taklon:
#4 and #10.flats: *LC 7300 or JS 1375*
#2, #4, #6, #8 filberts: *LC 5700 or JS 1385 sizes*
#3 round: *JS 1355 detailer or #2 or # 3 Raphael quill, 16684*

SURFACE

Wooden footed tray, 18" x 10¾" by *Gayle's Art Enterprises*

OTHER SUPPLIES

See Basic Supplies, page 2
Magic transparent tape
Jo Sonja's All-Purpose Sealer
Jo Sonja's Mediums: Retarder, Clear Glaze, Kleister, and Flow Medium
Jo Sonja's Polyurethane Matte Varnish or Blair Matte Spray

SOURCES

See page 127

INSTRUCTIONS

PREPARATION/BASECOATS

Sand tray and wipe free of sanding dust. Basecoat the top and bottom of the tray with Smoked Pearl + *All-Purpose Sealer* (3:1). Sand lightly. Apply a second coat. Add a little flow medium if too thick for a smooth, even coat. Sand loosely with 320-grit sandpaper.

Tape off the floor of the tray (top and underside) with magic transparent tape. Basecoat the routed rim (including underside and side edge) and also tray handles with Red Earth + *All-Purpose Sealer* (3:1). Sand and apply a second coat.

On the inside edge of the rim (next to the floor of the tray) apply a thin even coat of retarder. Sideload into dark red mix, Brown Madder + Burnt Umber, and apply so the darkest area is next to the floor of the tray. When dry, remove tape.

Basecoat the feet and handle holders with Teal Green + *All-Purpose Sealer* (3:1). Sand and apply a second coat. Allow to dry thoroughly.

Trim the outside edge of the rim top with Teal Green triangles. Lay a #10 flat brush at a 45° angle to the edge and pull the stroke towards the edge so it creates a triangle. When dry, extend the Teal Green color to include ⅛" at the top of the routed side edge. On the inside edge of the rim top, use a #8 filbert with Yellow Oxide and paint strokes about ⅜" long, pulling toward the inside edge. Paint inside the beaded area on the side of the rim with Teal Green. When dry, antique the entire beaded area with a dark red

color, Brown Madder + Burnt Umber.

Shade around the edge of the floor of the tray with a thin amount of Raw Sienna + Brown Earth. Apply a wide strip of retarder with a basecoating brush. Sideload into the shading color and apply with the darkest color next to the edge of the tray. Treat the underside of the tray in the same way. Dry thoroughly, then apply a coat of *Clear Glaze* to protect the entire surface.

SUGGESTED METHOD

Palette: I like to use a wet paper towel inside a folded piece of deli paper for a palette. Make sure the deli paper sticks down to the paper towel; smooth out the air, no wrinkles. This keeps the paint wet a long time. Dampen the paper towel if the paper starts to curl and dry. Cover when not in use. Prepare the following dark, medium, light paint mixes:

Red: DK = Burnt Umber + Brown Madder (1:1)
M = Red Earth
LT = Red Earth + Warm White

Yellow: DK = Raw Sienna
LT = Yellow Oxide

Green: DK = Teal Green
M = Green Oxide + touch Red Earth to soften
LT = Medium Mix + Yellow Oxide

Blue: DK = Storm Blue
M = Storm Blue + Warm White
LT = Medium Mix + Warm White

I like to tip my brush in *Retarder*, wipe gently on a paper towel, then load the brush. The paint blends nicely and doesn't dry too quickly. Load the retarder every 3-5 times you load the brush. You can tell when it needs more. If you get too much, the paint will be uncontrollable. Weather conditions also affect how often and how much you may need. Experiment; mix in some *Kleister* medium if you want a more transparent effect or the paint isn't working smoothly. I especially like a little *Kleister* in the Warm White for the overstrokes on the roses.

Transfer the pattern on page 68, centering it on the tray (see "Transferring the Design," page 7). Tape off the pattern area, if desired.

PAINTING
Center Motif
Use a #10 flat brush to paint the large outside square of the center motif with Yellow Oxide sideloaded into Raw Sienna. Use a #4 to paint the inside yellow square with Yellow Oxide. Fill in the triangles with Red Earth. Let dry, then paint a dark red line through the center of each triangle. When dry, load retarder in the #10 flat brush and sideload into Teal Green. Paint over the large yellow square, keeping the green to the inside of the square. When dry, use a #8 filbert with Teal Green to paint small arched strokes over the outside yellow band (nine strokes on each side of the square). On the red triangular areas, use a # 2 filbert to paint the strokes from the outside toward the center dark red line, following the shape of the triangle. Paint a Teal Green line between the red and green, if needed. Outline the inside yellow square with Raw Sienna + Brown Earth + *Flow Medium*.

Rosette
Paint the inside of the cup using a double-loaded brush in Raw Sienna and Yellow Oxide. Below that paint a half cir-cle of medium red mix for the cup. Paint the petals at the outside of the cup with light red mix, sideloaded with Warm White, using a #4 flat brush. Below these add the green leaf strokes, using a #2 filbert and following the instructions for the leaves below. Detail later as shown on the worksheet.

Roses (Large and Medium)
Paint the yellow band across the back of the rose with a double load of Raw Sienna and Yellow Oxide. Paint the inside of the cup with medium and dark red, keeping the dark to the bottom. Paint the front of the cup with the same values, dark at the bottom. Use dark red to paint two outside petals, using a #8 filbert. With Warm White + some *Kleister*, paint the five front petals over the wet red paint. I like to paint the green leaves next over the red petals while wet, but you may choose to let it dry.

For the two large roses, add a halo of 10–12 strokes above the yellow band, curving out from the center. Add side petals at the base, sideloading in light red mix + Warm White, then finish with two small circles of Raw Sienna + Yellow Oxide between the petals. For the medium rose, add just one yellow circle.

Daisies
Many of the flowers are painted with a front-on view, meaning the centers are round and the outside petals radiate out around them. For the yellow daisies, paint the yellow center with Raw Sienna and Yellow Oxide. Yellow daisies surrounding the center motif have an additional small red circle at the very center. Paint the petals with Warm White "igloo" strokes, pulling from the outside toward the center with a filbert brush. Paint groups of three light-green teardrops between the petals on the center motif daisies.

Paint red daisies in much the same way with the yellow center first. Sideload in light red mix and Warm White to paint the five petals, keeping the red to the center. Place smaller petals around the center using Red Earth and a small filbert, then add the tiny teardrops with dark red and the #3 round, following the contour of the petal. Paint the red daisy in the center motif in the same way except add a Red Earth ring around the yellow center and also a tiny Teal Green scalloped border around the outside of the ring (see worksheet, opposite).

Blue Flowers
Paint the ballflowers with dark blue on one side and light blue on the other. The lighter color should be facing the center motif. Overstroke the four petals at the base of the flower with dark blue. Paint yellow leaves above the blossom with a double load of Yellow Oxide + Raw Sienna. Paint leaves in two strokes with Raw Sienna to the inside or center.

Blue Leaves
While you are painting the blue ball-flowers, paint the blue leaves at the base of the medium roses, darker on one side as shown on the worksheet. Paint the small blue ballflowers at the tops of the large roses using light blue and a round stroke. Add the side petals by over-stroking the outside edges with middle value blue.

Red Buds
Load a #5 filbert with light red, lay the back of the brush, close to the ferrule, in Red Earth, and tip the brush in Warm White. Tap the brush on the palette to soften colors together. Make a teardrop so the dark part of the brush is at the stem end. Start at the tip of the bud, gradually push down as you pull toward the stem. Stop and lift. Detail with dark red lines.

Leaves
Use three values of green to paint the

Os Rosemaling

Palette

Storm Blue + Warm White

Teal Green

Green Oxide +touch Red Earth

+ Yellow Oxide

Burnt Umber

+ Brown Madder

Red Earth

Brown Madder + Burnt Umber

Raw Sienna

Yellow Oxide

Warm White

Daisy Centers

Red Daisy Petals

Yellow Daisy

Petal Strokes

Leaf Strokes

Red Buds

Blue Ballflowers

Blue Ballflower

Rose Centers

Rosette

Large Rose

Filler Flowers

Large Rose Detail

Blue Ballflower

Yellow Daisy

Red Daisy

Yellow Daisy

Rosette Detail

Red Daisy Center Motif

Filler leaves

Gram © 2002

1. Start with center motif. Paint color by color as numbered.
2. Paint flowers with strokes as numbered.
3. Add detail.
4. Add stems and fill-in detail.

67

leaves. Sideload into more yellow where desired. Some leaves require two strokes, (more rounded leaves), others are one, painted as a big comma or "S" stroke. Painting leaves with two strokes allows for more value change. Sideload into more Yellow Oxide for lighter leaves such as the leaves above the rosettes. Use Raw Sienna + Yellow Oxide and the #3 round to make tiny strokes along the edges of these leaves (see worksheet). Leaves for the large and medium roses should be darker. The small leaves can be painted with light and medium green. Paint yellow leaves above the blue flowers using Raw Sienna + Yellow Oxide. Paint yellow fill-in flowers using the same color. Detail the leaves as shown on the worksheet.

Stems and Fill-in Leaves/Flowers

Thin both the medium green and Yellow Oxide with *Flow Medium*. Paint the green or yellow stems, sometimes adding some Raw Sienna, or use a line of Raw Sienna for shading. There are fern-type leaves painted with just a line coming off a graceful stem, or there may be comma-like strokes or teardrops. Use a variety of strokes, greens and yellows. Use these to help balance color. At the same time, paint the veins in the leaves using Teal Green. White strokes may be placed between the dark veins on the light side, Yellow Oxide on the dark side.

DETAILS AND FINISHING

Use the #3 round for detailing, which includes dots on flowers and leaves; decorative patterns and linework on flower centers; outlines on flower petals, as well as added tiny filler flowers and stems. Use the darkest value of the color to detail the dark values. Use Warm White for light details. Refer to the photograph and worksheet as a guide to detailing.

Let dry thoroughly. Apply several coats of *Jo Sonja's Polyurethane Matte Varnish* or *Blair Matte Spray*.

About Marsha Weiser

Taking delight in fooling the viewer's eye, Marsha Weiser specializes in trompe l'oeil designs so realistic that they beg a second glance. A beginner's rosemaling class at the local YWCA, taken more than 20 years ago on a whim, provided the unexpected foundation of Marsha's painting career which previously had been pointed in the direction of her college mathematics major. Many painting classes later, and with the knowledge that comes from self-instruction and practice, Marsha now finds herself sought after as a designer and teacher. She began teaching in several local shops in her Brewer, Maine, locale. This led to the opening of "Maine Country Painting," a decorative painting shop which she ran for seven years. She closed the shop in 1994 because designing and travel-teaching began to consume most of her time.

A member of the Society of Decorative Painters for many years, Marsha became a Certified Decorative Artist in 1990. She now paints exclusively in acrylics, though someday hopes to get back to oil painting. She specializes in still life, especially trompe l'oeil painting with the dramatically realistic look. Country landscapes with lots of detail and a New England flavor are also favorite subjects for her paintings. She has written six decorative painting books: *Realistic Illusions, Vols. I* and *II; Scenes from Back Home, Vols. I, II* and *III;* and *Put It in Perspective*. She has designed over 75 design packets as well. She successfully authored a series of magazine articles teaching painters how to "see" their subjects in the dimension and depth necessary for achieving realism. Marsha's trompe l'oeil cutting board design on page 77 will add a touch of levity to your kitchen countertop. Can't you just see your family trying to snack on these mushrooms and tomatoes?

Tromp l'oeil painting often makes the viewer laugh, either by the choice of subject matter or merely by the fact that the viewer has been fooled into believing the painted objects are real. To achieve this effect, objects must be placed in a natural, logical setting like cups on a shelf or strawberries in a basket.

Trompe L'Oeil

By Marsha Weiser, CDA

TROMPE L'OEIL (PRONOUNCED TROMP LOY) SIMPLY MEANS FOOL or trick the eye. I like to think of it as the art of the second glance. If done well, it isn't even noticed at first glance. It appears so realistic that it seems perfectly natural in its setting. However, on second glance, the illusion is revealed. The intention of a trompe l'oeil painting is to deceive, even if only briefly. Sometimes the illusion holds up longer, causing the viewer to question just what is real and what is painted. About the highest compliment a trompe l'oeil painter can get is to have someone need to touch the painting because they can't trust their eyes.

What makes a trompe l'oeil painting different from other paintings? The most important thing, of course, is *realism*. The objects in the painting must be realistic in size, color, shape, and texture. Apples with a blue tinge may work in the color scheme of a still life, but they will not fool anyone into thinking that they are real apples. Likewise, an apple the size of a watermelon can make a dramatic statement, but that statement is not about reality!

Objects must be placed in a natural, logical setting. Books sitting on a shelf are logical, as are strawberries in a basket. A strawberry sitting on a bookshelf is out of place and unrealistic. A vase of flowers can be painted on a wall and shaded and highlighted realistically so that it has a terrific three-dimensional look. However, if there is no corresponding shelf or table painted below it to support it, the realistic effect is lost.

The objects in a trompe l'oeil painting are usually common, everyday items. They may fit into a particular theme and may even tell a story of sorts. There is sometimes a sense of mystery in a jumble of objects painted in a cabinet or on shelves. Why were these particular items chosen? How do they relate to each other? Half-hidden objects can also add to this mystery. A trompe l'oeil painting often makes the viewer laugh, either by the choice of objects or merely by the fact that the viewer has been fooled into believing it's real!

How does a trompe l'oeil painting differ from a realistic still life? A still life, no matter how realistically painted and how much depth portrayed, is not truly a trompe l'oeil if it is not self-contained. A still life is usually framed, with parts of the subject (the table for example) cut off by this frame. This spoils the illusion of reality. Everything in the trompe l'oeil painting must be complete with no cut off edges. Still life are also not always painted life-size, which a true trompe l'oeil must be to be effective. Because of these limitations, it can be said that every trompe l'oeil is a still life, but every still life is not a trompe l'oeil.

PAINTING A TROMPE L'OEIL DESIGN

Whether drawing your own design or using another's pattern, you can create a trompe l'oeil painting by working through the following steps. These are basically the same steps you would use to paint a still life, with extra emphasis on depth and dimension and keeping in mind the requirements of trompe l'oeil.

Plan Your Design

There is an infinite number of subjects to paint in the trompe l'oeil style. Just look around you and think about how you could "fake" the things you see. You can create cabinets and shelves for the walls, paint covered boxes to look like they are open and full of things, even add architectural details like moldings or windows on blank walls. You will be more successful if you choose relatively shallow objects and spaces. It is more difficult to hold an illusion for great depth. No matter what you decide to do you will be using one of two techniques called *evasion* and *invasion*.

Evasion means that you are creating the illusion of space behind the flat surface you are working on. When you paint a cabinet door to look like open shelves

you are using evasion. The painting surface is the foreground of your picture and the objects you paint are set into it.

Invasion, on the other hand, has the painting surface as the background and objects appear to stick out from this surface towards the viewer. A slightly opened drawer or a book overhanging a table edge are examples of invasion. To get the maximum illusion of depth it helps to use both invasion and evasion in a design if possible.

Choose Your Surface

Sometimes you may choose a painting surface first, and then decide what you want to paint on it. Other times you may know what you want to paint and you need to find the right surface for your painting. What you choose will depend on your subject matter. Plain flat boards can easily become open shelves. Cabinets with flat doors (no molding) beg to be painted as cabinets with no doors. Sometimes the best thing to do is paint directly on the wall.

Any box that has a flat cover works as an open box filled with whatever you choose. Boxes also have sides that can be painted as well to give a secondary illusion seen from a different angle. Paint lettering on it and distress it and it becomes an antique advertising box. Or you can paint the sides to look like a woven basket. Use your imagination.

Establish the Eye Level

One cannot paint realistically without a basic understanding of perspective. Perspective is simply picturing objects to show relative distance and depth, creating a three-dimensional illusion on a two-dimensional surface. How we draw the objects in the painting, how we shade and highlight them, and the cast shadows we add, are all ways we use perspective to create depth, and therefore realism, in the painting.

First we must determine how we (the artist and the viewer) are looking at the items in the design. Are we looking up at them, down on them, from directly in front of them, or from an angle? A trompe l'oeil painting has one particular viewpoint which will have the greatest impact. Seen from a different angle or position, the illusion is lost and the painting will appear flat.

We need to consider the surface we are painting on and how it will be displayed. Will it be hung on the wall (or painted directly on the wall) where it will be viewed straight on, or will it be displayed on a table and normally viewed from above? We must begin by establishing the eye level and position of the viewer.

The eye level is simply the horizontal line that intersects your line of vision as you look straight ahead. If you are standing, you establish a higher eye level. Sitting down changes this eye level to a lower one. Looking to the left or right doesn't change the eye level, moving up or down does. Once you have decided what you want the eye level to be, it cannot change. Everything in the painting relates to this established eye level. Objects that are above eye level are looked up at. Those below the eye level are looked down upon. The shapes of the objects in your design depend on where you have set the eye level. A box, for example, will have a different appearance if you are looking down on it than it would if you were looking up at it. If you are looking down, the top will be visible, as well as the front and possibly another side. If the box is above eye level the top can't be seen at all. Cylinders and cone-shaped objects will change as well, according to the eye level. The only exception to this is a perfectly round object, which will appear the same no matter what angle it is viewed from.

In addition to the eye level you have

to decide what you want the ideal position of the viewer to be. It is generally most effective, and easiest, to assume the viewer is looking at the design from straight on, rather than from the side at an angle. Again, this viewing position will have an effect on the shapes of the objects. Where the eye level effects how much of the tops or bottoms are seen, the viewing position effects what sides are in view. With a central view, those objects to the left of the center of the design will show their right sides. On those to the right of center the left sides will show.

Check the Pattern for Accuracy

To put the elements of a design into proper perspective, accurate drawing is required. Nothing detracts from the realism of a design more than wobbly lines, whether straight or curved. Vertical lines need to be parallel to each other and perpendicular to the table or shelf where they rest.

Horizontal lines that are in reality parallel to each other appear to get closer together as they move back into the picture. This is because objects (and the spaces between them) look smaller at a distance than they do up close. For example, consider the edges of a book placed at an angle in the design. The thickness of the book in the corner closest to the viewer would appear fatter than the thickness of the back corner, which is farther away from us.

Cylindrical objects must also be drawn in proper perspective. A circle seen in perspective is an ellipse. Therefore the top and bottom of a cylinder will be ellipses. The farther away an ellipse is from the eye-level line, the fatter it is and therefore the more curve it has. Painting smooth ellipses that are the same on both ends is always a challenge!

Before going on to painting your design, check to make sure that both sides of the objects are symmetrical if that is your intent. It's also a good idea to draw in "hidden lines"—the parts of the objects that we can't see. This way you can tell if you have crowded things together too much and objects are trying to occupy the same space.

Establish the Light Source

Shading and highlighting will give form and depth to the painting. To get the maximum three-dimensional look required for an effective trompe l'oeil painting you need to exaggerate the lights and darks. One way to do this is by assuming there is a strong, close light source, which will emphasize the contrasts and create heavy shadows. Putting light objects on a dark background (or vice versa) is another way to increase the contrast and make objects come forward towards the viewer.

Choose a light source that will cast interesting shadows from one object onto another and onto the background. If you know where the painting is going to be displayed, it is even more effective if you can use the actual dominant light source for that setting. Once you have decided on the light direction make sure you are consistent throughout the painting. A change in the light source in the middle of a painting is very confusing and will spoil the realistic effect you're trying to achieve.

Basecoat

Once you have your design planned and transferred, you can begin painting! When basecoating, use two or three thin coats of paint rather than one thick one. It should be smooth with no visible brushstrokes. Keep the edges crisp and even. This is sharp focus painting.

Shading and Highlighting

Body shadows are the dark areas that occur on an object in areas away from the light. *Highlights* are the light places where the light directly hits the object. It is the contrast between these lights and darks and all the variations of values in

You have to look twice to realize that this basket filled with crayons, markers, and scissors is actually just a flat oval box painted on the side to look like a woven basket.

between them that give an object its shape and volume.

A gradual change in value makes a flat surface appear rounded. A sharp value change—light directly against dark—creates an edge or corner. Shading is done with floated color (sideloading) or with washes. Highlights can be put in with dry brushing or with floated color. Both shading and highlighting should be done with thin layers of paint, building up the value changes gradually. Each layer is smaller and darker (for shading) or lighter (for highlighting) than the one before it. This is the step where your painting really begins to take shape and have some depth.

Add Details

Rust on an old tin piece, wood grain on a knife handle, or seeds on a strawberry—these are the details that make your painting life-like. Some may be put in before the shading, others after. If they are put in after, make sure to shade and highlight the details themselves. No matter how hard you have worked to make a round jar look round, putting an unshaded label on it will flatten it and spoil the effect.

The extra little details have the added benefit of holding the viewer's interest after the "first glance" illusion is gone. They are the little surprises that are only noticed with longer examination of the painting.

Add Cast Shadows

A *cast shadow* is the effect one object has on another because it is between the light source and the second object. The cast shadow's shape depends on the shape of what is casting it, the shape of what the shadow lands on, the distance between the objects, and the angle of the light source. Shadows help us understand the position of the objects in the design, as well as the size and shape. They are a very important part of the overall design.

With the strong, close light source we have chosen, these shadows will be dark, dramatic, and slightly exaggerated. They will have definite edges as opposed to fading away gradually. Put the shadows in with washes of thin paint so that they will be slightly transparent. The color used for the shadow will depend on the color of the object on which it lands. Therefore, one shadow that falls on several items will change color accordingly. Cast shadows also have value changes within them. Darken them by shading next to the object casting the shadow. This is really an important step—you will be amazed at how much depth it adds to your painting.

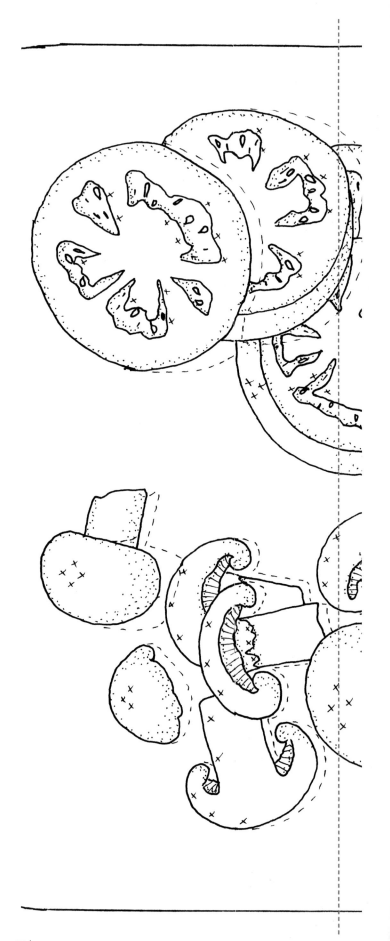

74

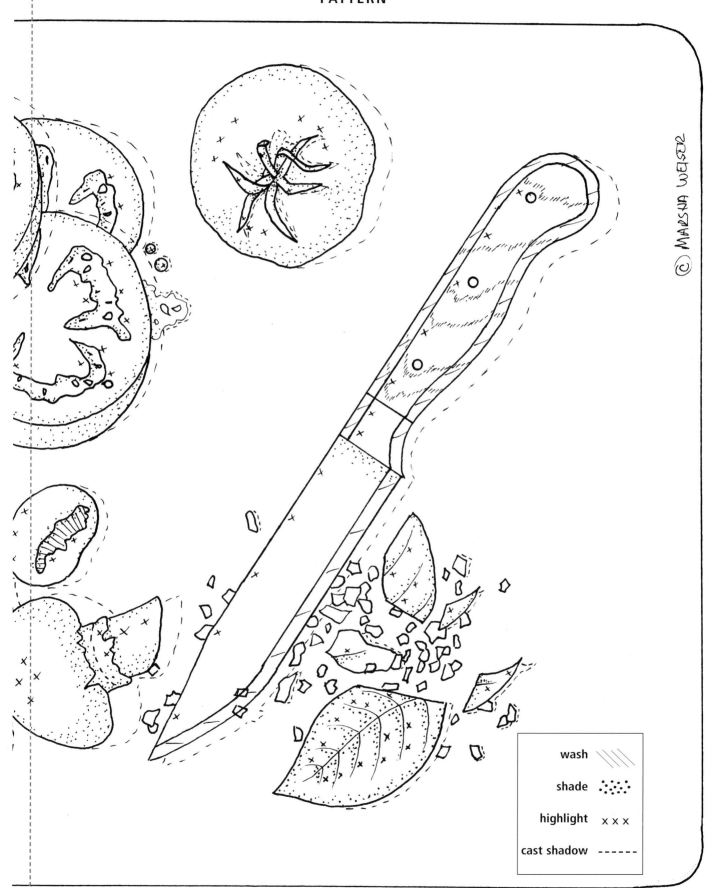

wash	/////
shade	:·:·:·
highlight	× × ×
cast shadow	- - - - - -

© MARSHA WEISER

Salad Fixings

Designed by Marsha Weiser, CDA

MATERIALS

PALETTE
Delta Ceramcoat Acrylics:
Black *Licerice*
Burnt Umber
Cadet Gray *Dove Grey*
Dark Forest Green *Island Pine or thicket*
Desert Sun *Gingerbread or wh, with*
Light Foliage Green *Houser Lt. g.s green*
Maroon *Black Cherry*
Medium Foliage Green *Hauser med.*
Poppy Orange *Autumn Leaves*
Putty *wh. with #R5*
Spice Brown *Nutmeg*
Straw *Buttercup*
Territorial Beige
Tomato Spice
Trail Tan *Butter Pecan*
White

BRUSHES
Loew-Cornell Golden Taklon:
#3 round: *Series 7000*
#6, #8 flat shaders: *Series 7300*
#00, #6 liners: *Series 7350*
⅜" angular shader: *Series 7400*
¾" flat wash: *Series 7550*
⅛" deerfoot stippler: *Series 410*

SURFACE
Hardwood cutting board (9" x 17" including the handle); design area 7½" x 9¾"

OTHER SUPPLIES
(See Basic Supplies, page 2)
Delta Ceramcoat Satin Exterior/ Interior Varnish

SOURCES
See page 127

INSTRUCTIONS

GENERAL DIRECTIONS

This particular cutting board is made by Farberware, and was purchased at a discount department store. Most stores that have a kitchen department will carry a similar board. The vegetables in the design can be moved around to accommodate a slightly different board.

All basecoating is solid unless otherwise noted; use 2-3 coats of paint for good coverage. Use an angular shader and floated (sideloaded) color for the shading (see Sideloading Color, page 11). A flat brush may also be used, if you prefer. Generally use two or more layers of color. Each layer is smaller and darker than the one before. Float the highlights also in layers, each one gradually lighter and brighter than the one before it. Circular highlights (on a mushroom cap, for example) are done by pivoting the brush, keeping the corner of the brush with the loaded color in the center at all times. Add the final highlights with a touch of stronger White. Refer to the pattern for the placement of the shading and highlighting.

Paint the cast shadows with washes, using a #6 liner. A smaller liner brush is necessary for the tiniest shadows. When doing washes, thin the paint with water. Make sure to blot the brush on a paper towel after loading it with paint so that you are using a damp brush with a scant amount of very thin paint. If you find you are getting streaks or puddles, you need to blot the brush again. Shading next to the object that is casting the shadow deepens the shadow. The placement of the cast shadows is also shown on the pattern.

Note: The light source for this design is from an angle above the handle of the cutting board.

PREPARATION

The surface for this project is the back side of a purchased hardwood cutting board that needs no preparation. Transfer outlines only from the pattern on pages 74–75 (see "Transferring the Design" on page 7. Refer to the symbols (see key on page 75) for placement of washes, shading highlighting, and cast shadows as instructed.

Mushrooms

Basecoat with Putty, using a #8 flat. Using a ⅜" angular shader, shade the mushrooms with Trail Tan. Darken in places first with Territorial Beige and then Spice Brown. Add random dabs and streaks of the darker colors for bruises and texture. Highlight with White. The gill area is Territorial Beige shaded with Burnt Umber. Using a #00 liner, add tiny lines of Burnt Umber and Trail Tan. The cast shadows that fall on the mushrooms are washes of Burnt Umber, shaded with more Burnt Umber. (All shadows that land on the board itself will be added later.)

Tomatoes

Using a #6 flat and Poppy Orange, basecoat the outer skin, the fleshy ring and about halfway towards the center of the "spokes." The centers and the

remaining half of the spokes are Desert Sun. Double load a #8 flat with Poppy Orange and Desert Sun. Blend well on the palette and use to soften where the two colors meet on the spokes. Shade the skin (including the end slice) with Tomato Spice. Darken this shading in the deepest parts with Maroon. Shade around the outer edge of the fleshy rings with Tomato Spice. Highlight with Poppy Orange + Straw, then Straw, then Straw + White, and finally with White.

Pounce a scant amount of Poppy Orange and Tomato Spice over the centers of the tomato slices using a ⅛" deerfoot stippler. For more texture, add a few stronger dabs and streaks with these colors as well. Highlight with a little White.

Basecoat the juice and seed areas with a heavy wash of Tomato Spice, using a #3 round brush. This should have just a hint of transparency. Shade with more Tomato Spice and darken the shading with Maroon.

Paint the seeds with Straw. Some will show as a complete seed, others will appear as a tiny line or dot. The larger ones have a touch of Spice Brown for shading and a White highlight dot.

Basecoat the bracts on the end slice with Medium Foliage Green. Shade with Dark Forest Green and highlight with touches of Light Foliage Green.

The shadows cast by the bracts on the tomatoes and where the slices overlap each other are washes of Maroon. Darken the shadows with Maroon shading. A tiny touch of Maroon below the larger seeds sets them into the juicy area.

The drops of juice are very thin washes of Tomato Spice with a little Tomato Spice shading at the top. Float a scant amount of White on the lower edge. A White dot highlight near the top completes the drops.

Knife

Basecoat the handle with Burnt Umber,

using the #8 flat brush. The wood grain on the handle is made up of tiny parallel lines of Black. Wash a narrow band of Black around the outside edge of the handle to create the beveled edge. Highlight with Territorial Beige. The rivets are Cadet Gray with a tiny White highlight.

Basecoat the blade with Cadet Gray. The sharp edge of the blade has a very thin wash of Black for the beveled edge. Use a little heavier wash to create the edges on the section that joins the handle. Shade with Black. Highlight with White.

Basil

Basecoat the basil with Medium Foliage Green, shade with Dark Forest Green, and highlight with Light Foliage Green. A tiny line of thin Dark Forest Green creates a cast shadow where pieces of basil overlap each other. Use a thin Black line under the pieces on the knife blade for the shadows.

Remaining Cast Shadows

Apply all the shadows that are cast onto the background board with washes of

Burnt Umber. Everything casts a shadow. For the larger shadows, shade with more Burnt Umber next to the object casting the shadow.

Sign Your Work

Yes, sign your work, but not in the usual way. Nothing will kill an illusion faster than a signature in the lower right corner that screams "I am a painting!" Sometimes you can sneak your name in as part of the design, on a label or an envelope for example. If not, then sign and date it inside or on the back of the wood piece.

FINISHING

Varnish the painted side of the board with 2-3 coats of water-based varnish. Using a ¾" wash brush will give you a smooth finish. An exterior varnish provides extra protection from water damage. Leave the unpainted side unvarnished so that it is food-safe and usable.

It's best to display your board on a table or countertop. Hanging it up will destroy the illusion—the objects on the board would slide off!

Drops of tomato juice add to the illusion of these freshly cut juicy tomatoes. The cast shadows give them added dimension.

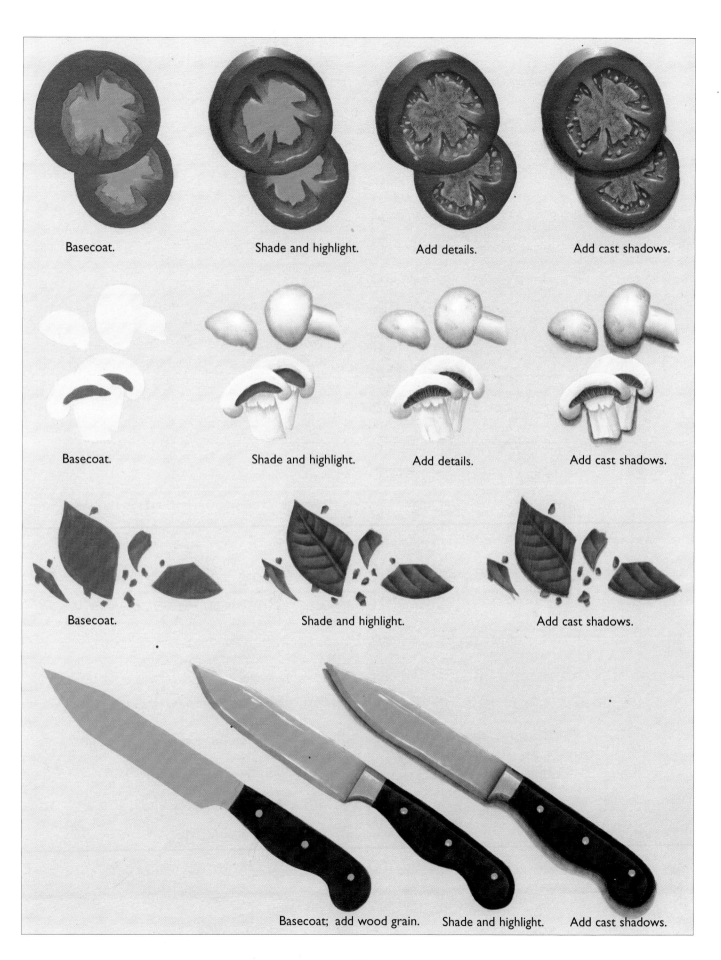

Basecoat.

Shade and highlight.

Add details.

Add cast shadows.

Basecoat.

Shade and highlight.

Add details.

Add cast shadows.

Basecoat.

Shade and highlight.

Add cast shadows.

Basecoat; add wood grain.

Shade and highlight.

Add cast shadows.

Capture the joy of a warm summer's day with this painter's mix of harvest-ready designs.

(below) An ivy topiary stands tall in a decorative wooden pot—a perennial favorite!

Adorn a painted shelf with pure country charm; this painted-plate collection serves up style.

(left) With a nod to nature, this bountiful round of painted fruit creates a colorful table top.

About Priscilla Hauser

Often called the "First Lady of Decorative Painting," Priscilla Hauser more than deserves the honor. Every member of the Society of Decorative Painters owes Priscilla a debt of gratitude for founding the organization in 1972.

Priscilla's interest in art was evident back in her childhood "crayon stage." The single most revealing story unfolded when she was 12: she envied a friend's new bedroom furniture adorned with hand-painted roses, in particular an old-fashioned camelback trunk. When she asked her parents for such a trunk, she received a plain, unadorned one and was told "Learn how to paint roses!" It was a challenge she took head-on, and she succeeded.

From that point success seemed to follow Priscilla in all her painting endeavors. Setting up a household as a new wife, Priscilla gravitated toward transforming old distressed furniture into small masterpieces through her decorative flourishes. Soon she was teaching others to paint, and before long publishing and travel-teaching at home and abroad. She now can list on her resume over 100 books (many on technique) as well as videos, magazine articles, and television programs. Her influence on the world of decorative painting, however, is incalculable. Priscilla has been showered with prestigious recognition: the Hobby Industries of America Hall of Fame Award "as a pioneer and innovator in the craft and hobby industry," the Priscilla Hauser Award for Business & Industry (created and named in her honor!), and selection with nine other painters from around the world by His Royal Highness Prince Bernard of the Netherlands to paint a panel for the Worldwide Wildlife Foundation. Which brings us to another of Priscilla's passions—animal rescue. As a guardian to several formerly abused dogs, she recently created "Angels for Animals," an organization which encourages people to donate money to worthwhile animal rescue organizations. Priscilla also donates a percentage of her book royalties to this cause.

Painting Fruit

By Priscilla Hauser

WHY IS FRUIT SO POPULAR? WELL, ACCORDING TO THE BIBLE, IT HAS BEEN there since the beginning. That tempting, gorgeous apple that Adam and Eve couldn't resist. Fruit is a joy. Not only is it good to eat, but it is beautiful. Its color can fall into any category you desire.

In Early American stenciling techniques, use of fruit is very apparent. Pears, peaches, plums, grapes, apples, melons, and berries are used on trays, Hitchcock chairs, and all sorts of tin surfaces—as well as many raw applications. Country tin painting began to develop in the late 18th century. In the 1930s and 1940s two wonderful artists, Peter Ompir and Peter Hunt, painted household items in wonderful colors. Their styles were completely different, but both artists featured fruit. Fruit is symbolic. For instance, the pineapple is a symbol of hospitality. The pomegranate symbolizes fertility. Even the early folk painters, who were not considered artists with their very primitive style, enjoyed painting fruit. This primitive painting is what I consider real folk art painting, and a primitive style is very charming.

So many different styles are created. For instance, an apple can be color-book painted and then antiqued or aged. An apple can also be created with brush strokes, or it can be blended in a wonderful realistic image. Remember, as you begin to paint, there are many ways of "right"—not just one. Have fun! That's what is important. It all boils down to creating a style you like and enjoy.

TECHNIQUES
Floating Color

There are as many different techniques for painting fruit as there are recipes for chocolate cake. However, a general rule of thumb when working with acrylics is to first undercoat the fruit with two or three coats of paint. Do this very neatly and smoothly. Let this dry and cure. Then a floating, blending, or glazing technique can be applied.

To apply shading and highlighting, use a method referred to as floating color:

1. Load a large flat brush with water or floating medium on one side and color on the other.

2. Blend on your palette to soften your color, so the color graduates in your brush from the pure color to the water or medium.

3. Apply the float in the proper area on your painting surface. This could be in the form of shadows or highlights.

Blending

This means to blend two or more colors together while they are wet. It is easy to achieve blending with oil paints. In fact, it is easy to over-blend because the oil paint stays wet so long. Acrylics don't stay wet long at all. That is why I like *FolkArt Blending Gel Medium*. It is a combination of extenders that helps the acrylic paint stay wet for a limited period of time.

1. Apply blending gel to the undercoated area.

2. Apply the colors to the subject you are blending.

3. Using as large a brush as possible and a very light touch, begin to blend or merge the colors together. More paint and/or gel may be needed.

Double Loading

Double loading is the skill of carrying two colors together in the brush at the same time with the colors gently merged together in the middle.

1. Place two puddles of paint on your palette. The paint should be the consistency of thick cream. Be sure the puddles are in proportion to the size of your brush.

2. Dip the brush in water and blot on a soft, absorbent rag.

3. Slowly walk the brush toward the lighter color and make contact with the edge of the color. Stroke many times (as many as 50), slowly edging the side of the brush into the paint. Don't press too hard or you will force the paint out of the brush instead of into the brush.

4. Slowly walk the brush over to the darker color. Put the other side of the brush into the darker color, stroking many times.

5. Blend the brush on the palette to soften the color. Blend many times on one side of the brush, then turn the brush over and blend many times on the other side. Pick up more paint if needed. The colors should blend beautifully together in the center of the brush. When you stroke, the color should flow from dark to medium to light.

Turn simple into stunning by adding lively fruit medleys to casual furnishings.
(right) Highlight a cozy chair to create a favorite reading nook.
(below) A tea tray becomes a feast for the eyes with a charming fruit motif.

**FRUIT FAVORITES
PATTERN**

Fruit Favorites

Designed by Priscilla Hauser

MATERIALS

PALETTE
FolkArt Artist's Pigments and Acrylics:
See chart below

BRUSHES
Loew-Cornell Golden Taklon
#2–#16 flats: *Series 7300*
#1 liner: *Series 7050*
¾" wash: *Series 7550*

SURFACE
Wooden chair, design area 14¼" x 4¼"

OTHER SUPPLIES
See Basic Supplies, page 2
FolkArt Glazing Medium
Masterson's Sta-Wet Palette
100% cotton rag or old T-shirt
Floating medium
C-Thru Ruler
Colored chalk
3M Magic Tape
FolkArt Clearcoat Acrylic Sealer—
Matte

SOURCES
See page 127

INSTRUCTIONS

I love the many wonderful variations of colors, styles, and techniques that can be used in the creation of fruit. I have chosen a floated method for apples, pears, pineapples, grapes, and leaves. It is a relatively easy technique with gorgeous results.

You can combine fruit with other fruit and flowers in so many different ways. I found this wonderful, old wooden folding chair at a flea market. It was already painted white and was slightly chipped and sanded in the shabby-chic style. Preparation could be anything you want, but I liked this chair just as it was.

If you follow the directions and paint along with my step-by-step worksheets, the results will be charming.

TERMS

Floating requires a double-loaded brush and floating medium or some other medium. This is applied on top of a dried undercoat to create shading or highlights.

Curing is more than just drying. Paint may dry on the surface but not yet be dry underneath the surface. No one can tell you exactly how long it takes paint to cure. It depends upon the color, the thickness, types of extenders used, room temperature, air circulation, and humidity. Most instructions give a maximum amount of time to be sure the paint is cured.

Double loading is carrying two colors of paint side-by-side on the brush. It is a technique that must be practiced and mastered.

PREPARATION

Paint the chair white (if it is not already painted) using any white acrylic of your choice. Let dry. If needed, apply a second coat to cover.

Sand, if desired, to take off paint here and there for a worn look. Wipe with a tack cloth.

Neatly trace and transfer the design on page 83 (see Transferring the Design, page 7). I trace my patterns with a pencil

Paints for Apple:	Paints for Pineapple:	Paints for Grapes:	Paints for Leaves:	Paints for Pear:
FolkArt Artist's Pigments:	*FolkArt Artist's Pigments:*	*FolkArt Artist's Pigments:*	*FolkArt Artist's Pigments:*	*FolkArt Artist's Pigments:*
Burnt Umber	Burnt Sienna	Prussian Blue	Hauser Green Light	Burnt Umber
Medium Yellow	Green Umber	Pure Orange	Green Umber	Raw Sienna
Napthol Crimson	Pure Orange	Titanium White	Pure Orange	Red Light
Prussian Blue	Raw Sienna	*FolkArt Acrylics:*	Titanium White	Titanium White
Pure Orange	Yellow Citron	Bluebell	True Burgundy	Yellow Citron
True Burgundy	*Folk Art Acrylics:*	Indigo	Yellow Citron	*FolkArt Acrylics:*
Yellow Citron	Bayberry	Porcelain Blue	*FolkArt Acrylics:*	Buttercup
FolkArt Acrylics:	Buttercup	Slate Blue	Bayberry	**Paints for Trim:**
Poppy Red				Asphaltum
				Yellow Ochre

on very thin, transparent tracing paper. On the back of your tracing, neatly go over the pattern lines with colored chalk. Never rub chalk all over the back of the pattern. Shake off the excess chalk dust. Position the pattern on the project surface. Secure with tape, if desired. Retrace the pattern lines with a pencil or a stylus. Don't press too hard. You don't want to make indentations in the wood.

Note: Paint the designs in the back or underneath first, building forward to the front of the design.

PAINTING THE DESIGN
Leaves:

Refer to the worksheet (opposite). Undercoat the leaves with Bayberry. Three coats will be needed to sufficiently cover the white. The undercoating should be as smooth and neat as possible. Let the paint dry between each coat. Once the final coat has dried and cured (24 hours minimum), apply a thin coat of glazing medium to the leaf.

Double load a large flat brush with glazing medium and Green Umber. Blend on your palette to soften the color. Apply the shadow to the base of the leaf.

Continue to apply Green Umber shadows to the left side of the leaves.

Double load the brush with glazing medium and Hauser Green Light. Apply this mixture to the remaining leaf edges as shown on the worksheet. Let the entire leaf dry and cure.

Using the glazing medium and True Burgundy, float a tiny bit of True Burgundy over the shadow area to create a bit of a burgundy accent. Using the same floating skill, float a highlight on the right side of the leaf with Yellow Citron. Let the leaf dry and cure.

Float a touch of Pure Orange on the right side as shown on the worksheet. Place a highlight of Titanium White.

Grapes
Dark Value Grapes

Using a small flat brush, neatly undercoat the grapes with Slate Blue. Apply three coats, allowing to dry between each coat. Dry thoroughly and cure.

Apply a thin coat of glazing medium to the grapes. Shade with a float of Indigo. Let dry and cure.

Paint a thin line of Pure Orange, as shown on the worksheet.

Medium Value Grapes:

Undercoat with Slate Blue. Paint with three coats to cover, allowing to dry between coats. Let dry and cure. Shade by floating on Indigo.

Accent the upper portion with a float of Bluebell. Highlight with Titanium White.

Light Value Grapes:

Undercoat with Slate Blue. Paint with three coats to cover, allowing to dry between coats. Let dry and cure.

Shade by floating on Indigo. Accent with Porcelain Blue.

Outline for Grapes:

Make a mixture of thinned Titanium White plus a tiny touch of Prussian Blue. Using a #1 liner brush, outline each grape.

Pineapple
Pineapple Leaves:

Undercoat the leaves with Bayberry. Three coats will be needed to cover. Let dry and cure.

Float on a shade of Green Umber. Highlight with a float of Yellow Citron.

PINEAPPLE

Undercoat leaves Bayberry; shade base GU.

Float left GU.

Highlight right YC.

Undercoat pineapple with Buttercup. Float RS on left and bottom. RS lines.

Float YC on right. Float GU top and bottom. Float RS in each "V."

Accent lower left with PO float. RS lines.

DARK GRAPE

Undercoat SB; shade Indigo; PO line.

MEDIUM GRAPE

Undercoat SB; shade Indigo; accent Bluebell; highlight TW.

LIGHT GRAPE

Undercoat SB; shade Indigo; accent Porcelain Blue; PB + TW line.

LEAVES

Undercoat leaves Bayberry; float GU to shade base.

Float GU on left. Float HGL on remaining edges.

Accent base TB.   Highlight right with YC.

Accent lower right with PO; upper right with TW.

87

(I sometimes add a touch of white to the Yellow Citron.)

Pineapple Fruit:
Undercoat with three coats of Buttercup. Let dry and cure.

Dampen the pineapple with glazing medium. Float Raw Sienna down the left side and across the bottom. A second and third float may be added for depth. (Sometimes I use a touch of Burnt Sienna mixed in with the Raw Sienna.) Let dry and cure.

Using a liner brush, paint the diagonal lines using Raw Sienna. Let dry and cure.

Float Yellow Citron on the right side. Create shadows under the leaves of Green Umber. Let dry and cure.

Float Raw Sienna in the "V" area of each section. Add accent lines of Raw Sienna in the "V" areas. Let dry.

Accent with a float of Pure Orange in the dark shadowed area. (***Note:*** *Anytime you wish to deepen a color, let the float dry and cure. Then float a second or third time, if desired.*)

Pear
Pear Fruit:
Neatly, carefully and smoothly undercoat

the pear with three coats of Buttercup. Let dry between coats. Let the paint dry and cure.

Apply a thin layer of glazing medium to the pear. Using a large flat brush, float Raw Sienna on the left side of the pear. (A beautiful float requires a large brush.) Let the paint dry and cure.

Apply a thin layer of Glazing Medium and float Yellow Citron on the right side of the pear. Let dry and cure. Repeat these floats two or three times, allowing the paint to dry and cure between these floats.

Using your large flat brush, apply a float of Red Light over the Raw Sienna for a touch of color. Let dry and cure.

Apply a highlight of Titanium White, blending it out on the edges. (Sometimes we refer to this as "losing the hard edge" of the highlight.)

Apply the point of dimension by floating on a mixture of Raw Sienna and Burnt Umber (1:1). When I do this, I turn the pear upside down and paint an "S" stroke. Let this dry and cure, repeating a second and third time if needed.

Pear Stem:
Using a liner brush, neatly and carefully paint the stem Burnt Umber. Let dry. A second and third coat may be needed. Highlight with Yellow Citron.

Apple
Undercoat the apple with Poppy Red. Three coats will be needed to cover. Let the paint dry between coats.

Using a medium flat brush, float Medium Yellow in the areas shown on the worksheet. This begins to create the dimension. Let the paint dry and cure. Apply a thin layer of glazing medium. Float Napthol Crimson on the left of the apple. Apply a "smile" of

Napthol Crimson under the yellow point of dimension (the point where the stem joins the apple.) Stroke the Napthol Crimson smile down over the yellow. Float Pure Orange on the right side of the apple. Let dry and cure.

Repeat the steps for the Napthol Crimson floats using True Burgundy. Deepen the point of dimension with a float of Prussian Blue. Be careful to use only a touch of Prussian Blue.

Fill the liner brush with thinned Burnt Umber. Neatly paint the stem with two or three coats to cover. Let dry thoroughly. Highlight with a thin line of Yellow Citron. A second or third coat may be needed to cover.

Trim
Using a pencil and a *C-Thru Ruler*, mark squares for the checkerboard design on the chair seat. (On this chair, I made 1⅝" squares.)

Float three light washes of Yellow Ochre in a pattern to make a checkerboard. Let dry and cure. Using a #16 flat brush, lightly float Asphaltum on the left and the right side of each yellow square.

Using *3M Magic Tape*, tape off a ½" border along the top and sides of the chair back. Float the border with two or three light washes of Yellow Ochre on the chair back.

With a #16 flat brush, float Asphaltum along the inside of the border on the white background.

Wash Yellow Ochre around the outside edge of the chair seat. When dry, float Asphaltum on the lower edge of the Yellow Ochre wash.

FINISHING
When thoroughly dry and cured, apply three light coats of a water-based varnish of your choice. Allow the varnish to dry between each coat.

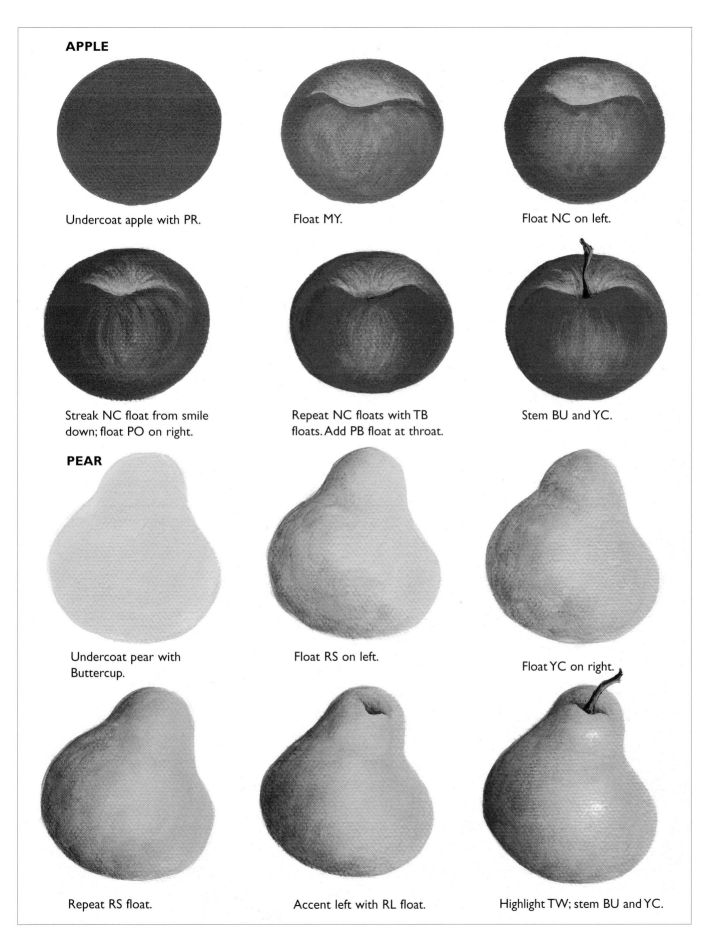

APPLE

Undercoat apple with PR.

Float MY.

Float NC on left.

Streak NC float from smile down; float PO on right.

Repeat NC floats with TB floats. Add PB float at throat.

Stem BU and YC.

PEAR

Undercoat pear with Buttercup.

Float RS on left.

Float YC on right.

Repeat RS float.

Accent left with RL float.

Highlight TW; stem BU and YC.

Flowers are decorative artist Arlene Beck's favorite painting subjects. The color or uniqueness of a flower generally inspires her realistic designs.

About Arlene Beck

"Since childhood I have had a love affair with flowers," Arlene Beck confesses. "I grow them, arrange them, dry them, and paint them. Flowers give me my greatest inspiration. I hope I can inspire you to find the joy I find painting flowers." In this Arlene succeeds admirably, from her floral "vision" to the way she inspires others through designing and teaching floral painting.

Arlene first began painting in oils, but made the shift to acrylics when they came into vogue. When she became acquainted with the certification program of the Society of Decorative Painters in 1985, it became her goal to participate in the program and pursue an advanced painting education. She studied and painted with as many accomplished artists as she could, attending conventions, as well as local chapter seminars. She painted her first certification board in 1986 and passed the last Master Decorative Artist level in 1995.

Arlene has written three books: *Gifts From My Country Garden*, *Gifts For The Fifth Season*, and *Painting Realistic Florals in Acrylic*. She also offers her devotees a line of over 75 pattern packets. Her quarterly newsletter on her Web page (www.arlenebeckmda.com) features unique and inspiring ways of living with decorative art, new packets, specials, and a question-and-answer column on teaching along with other aspects of decorative painting. Her desire to share her painting passion is obvious! Designing to teach continues to be Arlene's greatest objective. She travel-teaches nationally and internationally. She offers more intensive color and theory classes about four times a year in her home area of Duanesburg, New York, where she can also enjoy the pleasures of her garden.

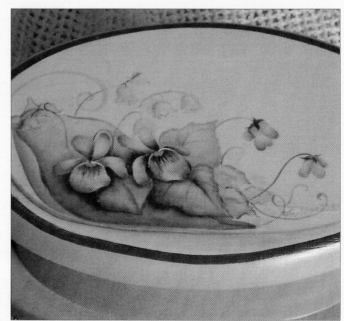

$\mathcal{P}ainting\ \mathcal{F}lowers$

By Arlene Beck, MDA

THERE ARE MANY STYLES TO CHOOSE FROM WHEN PAINTING FLOWERS. Included among them are folk art, impressionistic, whimsical, realistic, and a number of different decorative painting styles, some more realistic than others.

I have no one favorite flower that I paint; usually it is the color, or uniqueness, that inspires me. Flowers such as roses just lend themselves to being painted in different compositions. Someone once asked me "What was the most difficult flower for me to paint?" I have to say several things affect how easy a flower is to paint. For me it is much easier painting flowers if I like their color. Painting flowers that appear real, as they are in nature, are challenging. I want the petals to roll and fall naturally, the centers to look like the centers on the flower, and the leaves to be the leaves that belong to that flower. In some cases, as with multi-petaled flowers, I want to paint with detail, when it would be better to just give the illusion of many petals. The most difficult flowers to paint realistically become easier when I determine the basic shape and what value changes I will need to give the whole flower form. Once I have done that, I can work through the individual petals, painting them with the appropriate values for their position in that flower.

My style of painting is realistic. To make flowers look real they need form or dimension. To create form you need value change. Value is the lightness or darkness of a color. Three value changes are necessary to create a dimensional object on a flat surface. I create this dimension by painting gradual value changes from light value to middle value to dark value. Placement of these values is determined by the light source. In decorative art most paintings have an upper right center light source. To bridge the transition areas between light value and middle value and middle value and dark value requires good "blending skills." You may be proficient using water and floating color, like a dry brushed look, or prefer to use a painting medium to achieve this gradual change. I like to use *FolkArt Extender* to create gradual change in values.

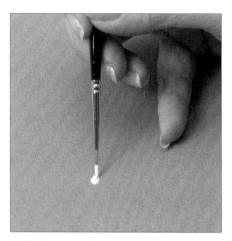

To lighten small areas, apply paint with a liner.

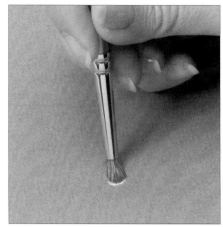

Apply pressure and force the paint outward using a domed brush.

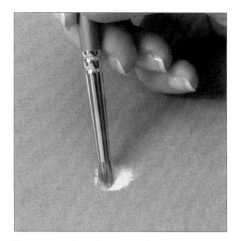

Soften until achieving desired effect.

Using Extender

Because water will dilute the extending properties of the extender, I apply the extender with a brush that I won't be using for painting and am careful to keep the brush out of my water basin. The extender can be rinsed out at the end of my painting session.

I apply a thin amount of extender on the surface; it does not matter if I carry it beyond where I will be applying paint. I want a sheen on the surface; I do not want to see brush marks or dry spots. To shade, I sideload my flat brush and apply paint in a pat and pull motion. Using long repetitive strokes similar to what I use when I float color would create a ridge along the outside edge. I use a "domed" round brush to soften paint into the background. I dry-wipe excess paint out of the domed brush in the damp area of my paper towel and avoid rinsing the brush until the end of the painting session. Once the painted area is dry, I can continue reinforcing the area, repeating the process.

Establishing Dimension

To establish the light value I extend the area and apply paint in an irregular star shape and soften with the "domed" round. If the light value area is very small, I will use a liner brush to apply paint, then soften with the "domed" round. Do not pounce the brush to soften, just apply pressure and force the paint outward. If you pick up excess paint while softening, dry-wipe the brush in the damp area of the paper towel and then continue.

When painting rolls or ruffles, I lighten the area I want to lift and shade in the area where the petal dips. If a petal is resting on a leaf or another petal I always choose to lighten the area where I can paint the most dark under, helping to lift the roll more. The decision is not as critical when there is just space behind or below the petal. One thing that is necessary to remember when painting rolls is that flowers generally do not reflect light or shine, and a very light value may cause an unnatural appearance.

Some things I consider when painting rolls, ruffles, or folds are length, width, and direction. Be sure all rolls are not the same length or width; make some longer, some wider, and some just on the edge. Think of the center of the flower as the gathering point of the flower, and when you paint the rolls direct them to the center.

Just as all the same shape and size of ruffles and rolls can be boring and uninteresting, the same is true for all the same color, value, intensity, temperature, and amount of detail.

The two most important colors on my palette are my main color, a cool pink in "Sweet Pea Jewels" on page 94, and my background color, blue-green. I use both colors throughout my painting to unify and help place objects on receding planes. On a light background, light flowers will recede into the background and the darker flowers will come forward. The opposite is also true, dark flowers will recede into a dark background and light flowers will come forward. I also keep in mind the value of the leaves and objects that touch or surround the flowers.

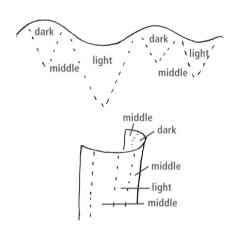

Create ruffles and rolls by placing light, dark, and middle values as shown (upper right light source).

Value of the leaves and flowers in "Sweet Pea Jewels" vary according to their position. Also the amount of value change within each flower and leaf varies according to their position. I tried to keep the upper bud and flowers close to the background value and with minimal value change within each. As I moved toward the largest center flower the value of the flowers become lighter as well as the amount of value change within the individual flowers. The largest flower has the lightest light values and the darkest dark values. The leaf behind the flower is darkest, forcing the flower forward and creating the greatest contrast between lights and darks.

Intensity, how bright or dull a color is, can also be used to help position a flower, petal, leaf, and help establish a focal point or just add interest. A color can appear more intense when next to its complementary color (the color opposite it on the color wheel). A color can be very dark or light and also very bright at the same time. There are times when a color does not appear intense until you have several coats of paint on a large area. If you are asking yourself if a color is too bright, you are asking if it is too red or too blue or too orange.

Intensity of a color can be altered by adding white, black, gray, its neighbor on the color wheel, a complementary color, earth color, or background color; with acrylic paint, water also dilutes the intensity.

In "Sweet Pea Jewels," the upper flowers are duller and fade into the background; the middle center flowers are the brightest especially along the edge. The lower flowers are a duller pink.

Temperature is how warm or cool a color is. Blue is the coolest color; orange the warmest. Every color has a warm and a cool side. Warm colors come forward and cool colors recede. Warm colors come forward on a cool background and cool colors recede, while warm colors recede on a warm background and cool colors come forward.

The middle center flowers are the warmest flowers. They have more yellow in their basecoat, lights and tints.

If a flower appears lifeless because I am using cool colors, I like to add a wash of a warm green. I use warm light values and avoid using white as a highlight value because it is so cool and can make a flower appear dead. Again, if this happens I will wash the area with yellow or warm green. Most flowers have warm yellow-green centers.

The top left leaves on the painting are cool, close in value and color to the background. As I move down and to the right side, the leaves become warmer and greener. The leaves around the larger more important flowers are darker, have warmer lights that are greener and carry more tints. The lower leaves are darker, but duller green. Value change in the leaves is kept to a minimum.

Details add interest and can help bring the viewer's eye to the center of interest and carry it through a painting. In this painting I used red tints on the leaves and tendrils, growth lines, ruffles, folds, and rolls on the main flowers. Keeping the detail linework on the box very close in color and value to the background prevents it from becoming distracting.

Notice also that there are just faint indications of flowers and leaves in the background.

"White Petunias" (above) was a challenge with its strong value change between the white flowers and the dark background. Using the background color throughout the painting kept the flowers from jumping off the background.

"Poppies and Gooseberries" was painted as a study in white. I used temperature to place objects throughout the painting. This piece is a high-key painting.

Sweet Pea Jewels

Designed by Arlene Beck, MDA

MATERIALS

PALETTE

Delta Ceramcoat Acrylics:

Bridgeport Grey	Rain Grey
Chambray Blue	Raw Linen
Custard	Rose Cloud
Dark Forest	Royal Plum
Green	Sandstone
Drizzle Grey	Sea Grass
Eucalyptus	Silver Pine
Flesh Tan	Soft Grey
Glacier Blue	Stonewedge
Ivory	Green
Leaf Green	Village Green
Lima Green	Violet Ice
Maroon	Wedgwood Green
Moss Green	White

BRUSHES

Loew-Cornell Golden Taklon:

#3 round: *Series 7000*

#4, #6, #8, #10, #12 flat shader:
  Series 7300

#2 liner: *Series 7350*

XS, S, M, L short "dome" round:
  Series 272

SURFACE

Wooden oval box with drawer,
  7" x 9¼" x 4¼" by *Country
  Pleasures*

OTHER SUPPLIES

See Basic Supplies, page 2
*Designs From The Heart™ Wood
  Sealer*
FolkArt Extender
Delta Ceramcoat Satin Interior Varnish

SOURCES

See page 127

INSTRUCTIONS

PREPARATION

Surface

Sand the wooden oval box with fine sandpaper, then tack the surface with a tack cloth. Seal the surface with *Designs From The Heart™ Wood Sealer*. Sand and wipe with a tack cloth. Apply one coat of Moss Green to the surface. Sand lightly and tack surface again.

Background

To create the mottled background, set out the following colors on your palette: Moss Green, Rose Cloud, Drizzle Grey, Violet Ice, Chambray Blue, Glacier Blue. Apply *Folk Art Extender* to the surface. ***Note:*** *If you are unsure of your ability to cover and blend the colors on the entire surface before the extender dries and colors start to set up, work in smaller areas, reapplying the extender as you approach the unpainted area.*

Apply background colors randomly, using quick irregular strokes and blending lightly as they are applied. Keeping the greener, duller, or gray colors to the lower left area and more of the lighter, warmer colors to the upper right and center area, apply the colors in any order using a large flat brush and blending as they are applied. Do not rinse your brush during the application of the paints; if necessary dry-wipe excess paint out of the brush onto a damp towel. Colors can be further softened together using a large "dome" round.

After painting the background, allow to dry thoroughly. The area should appear slightly blotchy with apparent hints of the different colors.

BASECOATS

Transfer the pattern on page 98 (see "Transferring the Design," page 7). Refer to numbers on the pattern to apply the following basecoats for flowers and leaves.

Flowers

1, 1A – Raw Linen

2 – Raw Linen + Sandstone

3 – Above mix + more Sandstone

4A – Flesh Tan

4B – Flesh Tan + Raw Linen (2:1)

4C, 4D – Rose Cloud

Leaves

1 – Silver Pine + Stonewedge Green

1A – Moss Green + Silver Pine

2 – Stonewedge Green + Drizzle Grey

3 – Moss Green + Drizzle Grey

4 – Wedgwood Green + Moss Green

5 – Wedgwood Green +Drizzle Grey

5A – Wedgwood Green + Bridgeport
  Grey

6 – Wedgwood Green

7 – Wedgwood Green + Drizzle Grey

8 – Stonewedge Green

9 – Eucalyptus

10 – Eucalyptus + Drizzle Grey

SHADING AND LIGHTING

Refer to the Shading and Lights diagram on page 99 for value placement. When two colors are listed, load both colors in the same corner of the brush and dress on the palette. All colors are listed in order of application, with each application covering less and less area.

Flowers

Shade the flowers before applying the red tints. The dark values are needed to support the darker red tints. Use only a scant amount of paint on the brush when applying tints. It is easier to reinforce than to remove paint that has been applied too heavily.

Flower 1

Shade – Chambray Blue + Stonewedge Green

Tint – Edge with Rose Cloud + scant touch Maroon

Flower 1A

Shade – Chambray Blue + Stonewedge Green

    Stonewedge Green + Bridgeport Grey

    Dark Forest Green + Bridgeport Grey (only in the tiny triangles under the bracts)

Lighten – Sandstone + White

Tints – Maroon + Moss Green more to the right side

    Maroon + Drizzle Grey to the cooler left lower side

Bracts – Moss Green + Drizzle Grey

    Shade – Eucalyptus + Bridgeport Grey

    Lighten – Moss Green + Soft Grey

Flower 2

Shade – Stonewedge Green + Drizzle Grey

Lighten – White

Tint – Maroon + Moss Green, keeping very faint

Flower 3

Shade – Stonewedge Green + Drizzle Grey

Lighten – Sandstone + White

Tint – Rose Cloud

Bracts – Stonewedge Green + Drizzle Grey

    Shade – Stonewedge Green + Bridgeport Grey

    Lighten – Stonewedge Green + White

Flower 4A

Shade – Stonewedge Green + Bridgeport Grey

Lighten – Raw Linen

    Custard

    White

Tint – Maroon

    Maroon + touch of Royal Plum, only in the darkest areas

Warm the center area of the flower with Custard + Sea Grass.

Line the edge of the petals with Maroon + Royal Plum, but do not make this a continuous line.

Flower 4B

Shade – Maroon + Sea Grass (3:2)

    Maroon

Lighten – Ivory

    Custard

Bracts – Wedgwood Green + Drizzle Grey

    Shade – Wedgwood Green

    Lighten – Wedgwood Green + White

Flower 4C + 4D

Wash both flowers with Maroon.

Shade – Maroon + Sea Grass

    Maroon + Royal Plum

Lighten – Raw Linen

    Ivory

Leaves

The leaves at the top of the painting are cool and light, helping to set them into the background. To cool a leaf, wash with Village Green. As I moved down to the right center area, the leaves became darker, greener and warmer. To warm a darker leaf, wash leaf with Leaf Green. To warm a light leaf wash light value with Lima Green. The leaves on the left side became darker but stayed cooler. The leaves surrounding the big flower are the darkest, warmest and greenest. Continuing down, the leaves become a duller green, slightly cooler, not quite as dark and carry fewer value changes.

Some leaves are lightened at the tip and shaded under the flower or at the stem, while others are lightened in the middle and shaded slightly at the tip and at the stem end to give the illusion they are bending. If a light value appears chalky, wash with Leaf Green. Paint the stems and tendrils with cool green colors and fade them into the background as they travel to the outside of the design. They have value change (darker at the edge and lighter in the middle) and some have Maroon tints to help carry the red color. Be sure some of the tendrils fall on top of leaves.

Leaf 1

Shade – Drizzle Grey + Dark Forest Green

Lighten – Soft Grey + Silver Pine

Leaf 1A

Shade – Stonewedge Green

Lighten – Raw Linen

Leaf 2

Shade – Stonewedge + Bridgeport Grey

Lighten – Stonewedge Green + Soft Grey

Leaf 3

Shade – Moss Green + Bridgeport Grey

Lighten – Moss Green + Soft Grey

Leaf 4

Shade – Wedgwood Green + Dark Forest Green

Lighten – Moss Green + Sandstone

Leaf 5

Shade – Wedgwood Green

Lighten – Soft Grey

Leaf 5A

Shade – Wedgwood Green + Bridgeport Grey

    Bridgeport Grey + Dark Forest Green

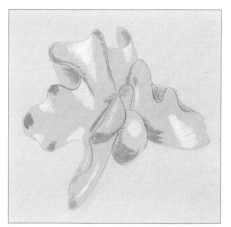

First value shade and light

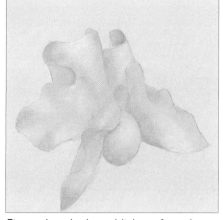

First value shade and light softened

Second value light; second value shade or tint

Leaf 6

Shade – Wedgwood Green + Dark Forest Green

   Dark Forest Green + Bridgeport Grey

   Dark Forest Green + Rain Grey

Lighten – Wedgwood Green + Sea Grass

   Sea Grass

   Custard

Leaf 7

Shade – Wedgwood Green + Bridgeport Grey

   Dark Forest Green + Bridgeport Grey

Lighten – Soft Grey

Leaf 8

Shade – Stonewedge Green + Bridgeport Grey

   Bridgeport Grey + Dark Forest Green

Lighten – Stonewedge Green + Soft Grey

Leaf 9

Shade - Eucalyptus + Bridgeport Grey

Lighten – Moss Green + Stonewedge Green

   Moss Green + Soft Grey

Leaf 10

Shade – Eucalyptus + Bridgeport Grey

Lighten – Moss Green + Soft Grey

FINISHING

Use the liner to paint a stripe ³⁄₁₆" from the top and bottom edge of the box. It should be dull and darker green than the background. You can adjust the green in the stripe to fade into your background by dulling it with Drizzle Grey, darken with Rain Grey, lighten with Moss Green or Soft Grey, blue the green with Bridgeport Grey. Apply a wash of darker green to the top scrolled edge of the wood piece and also to the outside edge of the oval lip at the bottom.

Finish by applying several coats of *Delta Satin Interior Varnish.*

SWEET PEA JEWELS
PATTERN

edge of box

knob

98

Red Tints (build gradually using several applications)

Shading and Lights

shade

lighten

99

"A beautiful landscape can pull you away from the present to another place and time," explains landscape artist Dorothy Dent.

About Dorothy Dent

Reared on a farm south of Springfield, Missouri, Dorothy Dent grew up amongst old barns, water mills, cabins, and rural settings, and her enduring love for these images is reflected in her paintings. Inclined to be artistic since childhood, she has been involved in the decorative art world for more than 30 years. Dorothy's studio and retail shop, Painter's Corner, Inc., is located in Republic, Missouri, just west of Springfield. Here she teaches workshops and week-long seminars throughout the year. As a teacher, she is known for her hearty encouragement for beginning painters and generous sharing of her extensive painting knowledge.

In 2000 Dorothy was named one of the "Top Ten Talents in the Decorative Painting Field." As a nationally recognized artist, she travels extensively in the USA, Canada, Argentina, Australia, and Japan. She has appeared on two 13-week PBS television series. She has self-published 27 books on landscape painting and authored the book *Realistic Landscapes.* She is a contributing artist and advisory board member for several painting magazines for which she writes instructional articles from time to time. She has produced more than 100 painting packets and a series of technique and landscape videos.

Dorothy's easy-to-follow, step-by-step instructions make it possible for even beginners to complete paintings with pride. Although Dorothy is best known for her work in oils, she also paints and teaches in acrylic. She enjoys working in both mediums, and her distinct style is easily adapted to both. The gracious old country house on Dorothy's "Tea House" caddy project on page 104 is typical of the country landscapes for which she has become so well-known.

Painting Landscapes

By Dorothy Dent

ART WORK FEATURING LANDSCAPES HAS ALWAYS BEEN ONE OF THE MOST popular forms of paintings. Landscape paintings of one style or another will fit the decor of every home. A beautiful landscape can pull you away from the present to another place and time. One often thinks of landscape painting as only paintings of skies, trees, rocks, water, and so forth. However, landscape can include paintings of buildings, boats, street scenes, and other subject matter which is surrounded by the natural elements of skies and trees, etc.

The first thing one must do when learning to paint landscapes is to learn to see. Of course, we have all seen everyday objects such as skies, trees, and buildings, all of our lives. But not until we begin to paint them do we realize that we do not know what they truly look like. We must look very hard, and observe carefully to see the colors on the grass, the way a branch turns away from the tree trunk, how a shadow falls on a wall, and the way things look differently in the distance from the way they look close to us. All of this information is out there before our eyes, but we must translate it to a flat surface in such a way as to make it have depth and appear believable to the viewer of the artwork.

Many landscape artists paint on location, finishing a painting or a sketch on the spot. Others take photos to use as reference material and do most or all of the painting in their studio. Whether you paint on location or from reference material, you still must decide on what to put into the painting, and what to leave out. To include all that you or the camera see would not only be next to impossible, but would also make for a very busy painting. You must decide what elements to include to make the statement you want. Consider what it is about this scene that makes you want to paint it. Is it the beautiful clouds, the nostalgic look of an old building, the interesting shadows of the trees on the ground, or the peaceful waterfall? Whatever it is that pulls you into the scene is what you want to emphasize. Add enough other objects in the painting to help "tell the story," and leave out the rest.

LANDSCAPE PAINTING ESSENTIALS

There are many ways to paint landscapes—from abstract to photo realism. Artist's styles will vary, and a style that is appealing to one person may not be to another. The guidelines below give some of the tried-and-true techniques that will help make your landscapes look more professional, no matter your style.

Sketching and Composition

The beginning of a painting is often a sketch. You do not necessarily need a detailed sketch, but you must determine where critical lines will be. In this way you will design the composition, and determine where the subject matter will be in the finished painting. You will decide what will be the focal point or center of interest. It is usually best to place that area just off center from the middle of the painting. You then need to add the other elements to balance out the painting.

There are rules of balance, but generally speaking you can look at a picture and "feel" if it is balanced or not. Are all the larger objects too much on one side? If so, they need to be distributed so that one side of the painting is not "heavier" than the other side. The picture will then feel more balanced, and not as if tipping to one side. Objects in the picture should not be lined up in rows. The scene will be more interesting if you do not see straight lines running from area to area.

It is a good idea to block in the light and dark values as you work up the composition. This will indicate how the finished painting would look in black and white, and be a value guide as you add color to the scene. To give depth to a painting, it is necessary to paint dark areas darker as they come forward. The lighter a dark value is, the farther away it seems. For instance, a group of pine trees in the foreground should be darker in

value than the same type of trees farther away. Light and dark values add depth and a feeling of perspective to a flat surface. You might try a small sketch of the painting on a piece of scrap paper. With a pencil, add light and dark values to see the composition as a value study. This could be referred to as you add color to the larger work.

Leading to the Center of Interest

As you work up your composition there are a few tricks to lead the viewer's eyes to the center of interest in the painting. After all, this is what you want the viewer to see. A winding road or stream of water will lead the eye into the painting. Point the end of the road or water into the painting rather than out of the painting. Other features, such as fences or tree branches, can also help to point in the direction of the focal point.

Once the viewer has been guided into the painting you do not want their eyes to leave the scene too quickly. For instance, if there is a straight line running directly out of the painting, such as a fence row, or the horizon line, the viewers eyes will zip right down that straight line, and out of the painting. However, you can block the line by pulling a bush, tree, or any other object across the line just before it exits the painting. In this way the eye will be stopped before it leaves the scene, and will return to the middle of the painting.

Light

The way light is portrayed will make or break the painting. A viewer is attracted to a painting mostly by the way the artist has used light and shadow. Dramatic lighting will only look dramatic if there is enough dark or shadowed areas to play up the light. Light will not be seen as light unless there are dark areas nearby to compare the light to. Many times stu-

dents fail to paint dark areas dark enough to make the adjacent light areas sparkle with sunshine.

There will always be a light source in each painting. Light will either come from the sky as soft light, or as direct rays of the sun slanting across the scene. The most dramatic light in a landscape can always be seen in the early morning or late afternoon when the sun's rays are slanting across horizontally. Artist's like to paint on location during these brief times, or take reference photos to remember how the light and shadow falls at those hours. When painting a night or late evening scene you may want to add light in the windows of a building. Again, you will think of how that light will illuminate the objects close to the windows, adding a spot of warm welcoming light to the building, and to the scene as a whole.

Be consistent with the light source in your paintings. Determine which direction the light is coming from, and make all objects that are catching the light bright on the same side.

Painting the brightest, most intense light area in the scene in close proximity to a very dark area is another good way to pull the viewer's eye into the focal point in the painting.

COLOR VALUE

Value is simply how dark or how light a color is. It is easy to see value when looking at black and white. When looking at color it can be a little more difficult to determine, in order to mix the proper value of the color in relation to where it will be placed in the painting. Most colors are lightened with the addition of white.

In all landscapes (except snow scenes), the sky is the lightest value in the painting, excluding man-made objects such as a white house. The sky being the source of light, it would be the lightest.

The next lightest value is the area of ground or trees that are the farthest in the distance. The dark values in this area will be a bit darker than the sky, and the other colors a bit more colorful, but still soft and hazy. As you come into the middle ground, the value of the darks will be a bit darker, and the value of the other colors a bit stronger. In the foreground the darks will be darker yet, and the colors brighter still. By using values in this way, you feel as if you are looking into the distance as you view the scene. Mixing the right color values takes practice, but is important for creating depth in your painting.

ACRYLIC VS. OIL LAND-SCAPE PAINTING

I love to paint in both oil and acrylic. There are advantages to both mediums, but the main advantage to working in acrylic is the fast drying time. I enjoy being able to brush thin glazes or washes of color on top of a dry basecoat to change the color, add highlights or shadows, etc. This is much easier to do in acrylic as the basecoat is dry in minutes. With oil you sometimes have to wait much longer. To correct a mistake in acrylics you simply paint over it again right away. There is no need to try to remove the paint as you might do in oils. Just paint on top of the "goof" and move on.

As I have been an oil painter for many years, I tend to work acrylics similar to oils in some ways. However, there are many areas where you cannot work acrylic as you would oil. With oil you normally work from dark to light on an area. With acrylic many times you must work from light to dark because of the fast drying time. For instance, on the tea caddy project in this book, you will begin the walls of the house with the light values, then wash the shadows in over the light walls. The fence and the road in front are done in the same way. The light will be painted in first, then the shadows applied with thin paint on top of the dry basecoat. It is mostly in the trees and bushes that I find I still need to begin with the dark basecoats and build up the light on top of the dark and medium values to get a realistic look.

ENJOY THE PROCESS

I like achieving a realistic look in my paintings, but do not feel that every line must be perfect. I like soft edges with a bit of an unevenness here and there. After all it is a painting, not a photo. I hope you enjoy painting the little tea caddy that follows. There are many small details in the scene—do the best you can, and if it isn't perfect, it's OK—perhaps it will have more character that way! The important thing is to enjoy the process. When all done, have a cup of tea, sit back and admire your work!

Light and shadow plays an important role in adding to the appeal of these paintings (above and right).

Tea House

Designed by Dorothy Dent

MATERIALS

PALETTE

DecoArt Americana Acrylics:
Antique Rose
Black Forest Green
Deep Midnight Blue
Green Mist
Golden Straw
Hauser Light Green
Light Buttermilk
Mink Tan
Payne's Gray
Pineapple
Russet
Salem Blue
Soft Peach
Titanium White
Violet Haze

BRUSHES

Royal Brushes:
#8 flat: *Series 150*
#4 filbert: *Series 170*
#1, #2 gold liner: *Series 595*

SURFACE

Wooden tea box, 6½" x 10½" x 4³⁄₁₆"
   by *Viking Woodcrafts, Inc.,*
      available from Painter's Corner

OTHER SUPPLIES

See Basic Supplies, page 2
Americana Brush 'N Blend Extender
J.W. etc. First Step Wood Sealer
J.W. etc. Right Step Satin Varnish

SOURCES

See page 127

INSTRUCTIONS

PREPARATION

Thin the paint with water when thin paint is needed. *Americana Brush 'N Blend Extender* may also be used if preferred.

Sand and seal the wood piece using *J.W. etc. First Step Wood Sealer*. When the wood is smooth, basecoat the front of the box with two coats of Titanium White. Transfer the pattern on page 108 using gray graphite paper (see Transferring the Design, page 7).

PAINTING PROCEDURE
Sky

Brush in the blue sky using the #8 flat and Light Buttermilk + Salem Blue. Vary the mix a bit so that some areas are lighter and some darker. Use short brush strokes with the flat of the brush, pointing in various directions. Brush in more Light Buttermilk for light clouds. When the sky is dry, brush in a little Soft Peach over some of the lighter clouds.

Background Trees

Working with the bottom corner of the #8 flat, pat in a basecoat of Green Mist + Salem Blue + a touch of Deep Midnight Blue in the distant trees. Pat in Hauser Light Green and Hauser Light Green + Pineapple + Light Buttermilk for light leaves. Extend some of the light leaves a bit beyond the basecoat so the sunlight will appear to be hitting the outside edges of the foliage. Leave some of the basecoat showing in the middle and bottom of the trees for depth. Add more of

the basecoat colors if too much has been painted over.

Paint the dark green background behind the blue wrought-iron grillwork to the right of the house. Pick up Black Forest Green + Deep Midnight Blue loosely mixed on the brush, and pat it in using the #4 filbert. Tap in a little Hauser Light Green for highlights.

House

Walls. Using the #4 filbert, base in the walls on the front of the house with Light Buttermilk. Also base in the right side of the dormer on the left. Base in what is showing of the left wall with Light Buttermilk + a touch of Deep Midnight Blue mixed to a light shadow color.

Thin this shadow mix with a little water and add a soft shadow line beneath the roof of the front gable end. Add the shading beneath the sign on the front, and beneath the fascia board above the lettering. When dry, add a very thin wash of Mink Tan—just a hint of tan is all you need. Paint the horizontal board lines on the house with the same blue shadow mix using the #1 liner. Get them as straight as you can, but if they are a bit off, don't worry—this is a painting, not a photograph. Add a little more Deep Midnight Blue to the shadow mix, and paint in the line beneath the overhang of the roof on the left side of the dormer.

After the linework is dry, brush over the entire wall with Titanium White using the #4 filbert. This will soften the board lines as well as add a whiter look to the house. The white is rather

SKY

Loosely brush in sky using Salem Blue + Light Buttermilk. Leave open areas for clouds.

Brush in the clouds with Light Buttermilk, overlapping the sky blues. Brush in more sky blues if needed to aid in blending.

When clouds are dry, glaze in a little Soft Peach by adding water to thin the paint. Brush lightly over the clouds here and there.

BACKGROUND TREES

Basecoat background trees with Green Mist + Salem Blue + touch Deep Midnight Blue. Pat in the general shape of the trees.

Add light leaves with Hauser Light Green + Pineapple + Light Buttermilk. Build the lightest foliage to the right sides of the clusters. Extend the light leaves beyond the edge of the basecoat.

HOUSE WALLS

Base the walls on the front of the house with Light Buttermilk.

Add shadows and linework with thinned Deep Midnight Blue + Light Buttermilk.

When dry, brush Titanium White over the wall to soften lines and whiten walls.

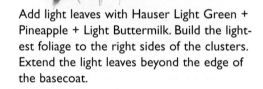

transparent so a little of the basecoat Light Buttermilk will still show through slightly to create a sunny look to the wall.

Paint the wall beneath the iron grillwork of the porch posts and trim with Deep Midnight Blue + a little touch of Light Buttermilk. Add some Payne's Gray to the left to create more contrast when the grillwork is completed.

Suggest a door behind the second post from the left with more Payne's Gray. Brush a few vertical strokes of Mink Tan inside the door. Highlight the right corner of the wall with Light Buttermilk, working with the tip of the #2 liner. Suggest horizontal board lines in the wall using the liner and Light Buttermilk + Deep Midnight Blue, mixing a color just

slightly lighter than the wall.

Wrought Iron Grillwork. Base the grillwork on the posts and top piece with Payne's Gray, using the #2 liner. When dry, use the tip of the #1 liner and Salem Blue for the grillwork. Paint small wiggly strokes with the tip of the brush moving in different directions. Add a little Light Buttermilk for highlights here and there.

HOUSE WALL BENEATH PORCH AND WROUGHT IRON GRILLWORK

Base in wall with Deep Midnight Blue + touch Light Buttermilk. Add Payne's Gray window and door suggestions. Highlight door with strokes of Mink Tan. Add corner board line and horizontal board lines with Light Buttermilk + touch Deep Midnight Blue.

Base in grillwork with Payne's Gray

Using the tip of the liner and Salem Blue + Light Buttermilk, make wiggly lines for the grillwork. Work for good contrast with the background. Brush in more thinned Deep Midnight Blue on the house wall if needed for contrast.

STEPS

Base in the riser part of the steps with Deep Midnight Blue + Russet. Leave a little line unpainted for the top of the steps.

ROCK WALL

Basecoat the wall with Deep Midnight Blue + Russet.

Add stones with Soft Peach, Soft Peach + Russet, and Violet Haze.

Add Violet Haze and Violet Haze + touch Light Buttermilk for the top of the steps, and for the sidewalk as it recedes back.

Add a light line at the top of the wall with Soft Peach + touch Light Buttermilk. Add Violet Haze in the shaded areas.

Work for good contrast with the background, tucking in more dark in the background, if needed.

Windows. Using the #2 liner, paint the window glass with Light Buttermilk + touch Deep Midnight Blue. Paint the pane lines Deep Midnight Blue, using the #1 liner. Add a dot of Light Buttermilk in a few of the panes for highlights.

Paint the shutters and the header above the windows Deep Midnight Blue + touch Light Buttermilk. Make small horizontal "shutter lines" with

thinned Deep Midnight Blue + Payne's Gray. Highlight a few with Light Buttermilk.

Roof. Paint the roof Russet + touch Soft Peach. Add more Soft Peach at the top of the dormer roof in the rear. Deepen the Russet on the lower left side of the front gable end next to the chimney with a touch of Deep Midnight Blue added to the mix.

Add a tiny line of Russet for the porch roof above the lettering and the fascia board.

Chimneys. Paint the chimneys

Russet using the #2 liner. Highlight the right sides with taps of Soft Peach to indicate small stones. Add a thin wash of Deep Midnight Blue over the basecoat on the left sides. Work for sharp contrast between light and dark at the middle corners.

Tea House Sign. Lightly pencil in the words, then go over them with the #1 liner and Deep Midnight Blue.

Fences

Paint out the fence by basing with a dark mix of Black Forest Green + Deep

TEA HOUSE
PATTERN

D. Dent

Midnight Blue. Add a few strokes of Hauser Light Green behind the left fence. Stroke the posts back in, stroking over the basecoat with the #2 liner and Light Buttermilk. When dry, brush in shadows with thinned Violet Haze. Highlight the lightest posts with Titanium White.

Bushes Behind Fences

With the #4 filbert and/or the #2 liner, tap in green mixed with Black Forest Green + touches of Green Mist. Add light greens and yellow-greens with Hauser Light Green, Golden Straw, and touches of Pineapple.

Paint the dark bush at the corner of the house Black Forest Green + touch Russet. Note that there are a lot of light greens and yellow greens beneath this bush and to the top of the fence.

Tap in a little Black Forest Green and touches of Hauser Light Green beneath the fence for grass.

Rock Wall and Steps

Base in the rock wall with Deep Midnight Blue + Russet using the #4 filbert. Suggest small stones with Soft Peach, Soft Peach + Russet, and Violet Haze. Work more Violet Haze in the shadow areas, and more Soft Peach in the sunlit areas. Add the light line above the wall with the #1 liner and Soft Peach. Wash a little thinned Violet Haze over it in the shadow areas.

Paint the risers on the steps with Deep Midnight Blue + Russet. Using the #1 liner, paint a line for the top of the steps, and paint the sidewalk going back with Violet Haze.

Large Trees

Base in the tree foliage with the #4 filbert and a dark mix of Black Forest Green + Deep Midnight Blue + Russet. Loosely mix the colors so sometimes there is more of one than the other.

Work for a loose irregular pattern to the edges. Add a little highlight foliage in the middle areas with Hauser Light Green. Tap it in over the dry dark basecoat. Limbs are threaded in and out with the #1 liner and thinned Deep Midnight Blue + Russet. Highlight with Soft Peach and Mink Tan.

Road in Front

Basecoat with Soft Peach. Brush in shadows with slightly thinned Violet Haze + touch Deep Midnight Blue. Pick up more Soft Peach as needed to aid in blending the shadows into the basecoat. With a slightly stiff small brush such as the #8 flat, flick in "gravel" with thinned Deep Midnight Blue. Simply rake your finger across the bristles while pointing the brush at the road. Keep the brush close to the surface so as not to spatter other areas of the painting.

Flowers

Tap in the little "roses" with the tip of the #2 liner using Antique Rose and Antique Rose + Light Buttermilk.

FINISHING

Basecoat all but the top of the box with two coats Soft Peach. Paint the top of the box, the edges of the back, and the edges of the bottom with two coats Black Forest Green.

Antique the Soft Peach using *Brush 'N Blend* + Payne's Gray brushed on with a soft brush, then rubbed lightly with a soft rag.

"Tea" Lettering

Transfer the lettering and the vine around it with gray graphite paper, centering it on the top of the back. Paint the vine, leaves, and lettering with the #1 liner and thinned Black Forest Green.

Varnishing

When all is done and dry, varnish with *J.W. etc. Right Step Satin Varnish*, or the varnish of your choice.

Vi Thurmond has a natural talent for capturing the "personality" of the animals she paints. She generally works from photos but uses reference materials to adapt photos to her design needs. This includes placing her subject in a surrounding that complements the animal.

About Vi Thurmond

When Vi Thurmond was learning to paint she sampled all traditional subjects: fruits and vegetables, flowers, and landscapes. But when she took her first portraiture class, she had a painting epiphany. This was what she was supposed to specialize in! "It was like opening a door!" she recalls. Instead of diversifying her subjects, she learned to specialize, and found her true niche.

Vi didn't discover her painting gift until she was well into adulthood. She has since dedicated herself to sharing her talent with others as an artist, teacher, author, publisher and businesswoman. She has authored six videos, seven books and developed over 150 instructional packets covering a variety of subjects and in a number of mediums. Her work has inspired countless decorative painters to create portraits of people and animals. Vi's designs have also appeared in numerous painting magazines. She has a line of 64 subjects in pet and country note cards, plus eight cat subjects on note pads. Recognized as a Master Decorative Artist through the Society of Decorative Painters, Vi maintains an active seminar schedule, teaching for retail shops, national and regional conventions, and affiliated chapters of the Society. She also teaches advanced portraiture classes in her Des Moines, Iowa, locale.

Vi is grateful to Glori Robison, her teacher who taught that first portraiture class years ago, as well as every other teacher with whom she's had the pleasure to study. Her advice to new painters is to take classes from as many teachers as possible: "You'll take a little something with you from every teacher."

Painting Animals

By Vi Thurmond, MDA

ALL FACES ARE UNIQUE. THIS OBSERVATION APPLIES NOT ONLY TO PEOPLE but also to animals. Once you paint an animal, you begin to see all the differences in animal faces. You notice different shapes and sizes of the features—even ears can be very different from one animal to another. I especially take into consideration the length of the hair/fur, its color, and the direction in which it lies.

When I began painting animals, I was so enthusiastic that I wanted to paint every animal in sight. I took photos of them, often shooting an entire roll of film while trying to get just the right pose—one that showed expression and revealed something about the "personality" of the animal. I've learned through experience to catch an animal while its mouth is closed (teeth have so many values and take entirely too much time to paint)! I make sure to start out with a good reference photo, one that makes both me and the animal's owner happy. I then enlarge the photo I've selected to 5" x 7" or 8" x 10", so I can see the animal's features more clearly and study the direction of the fur.

If you can't see as many details as you'd like in your photo, do some research at your local library or on the Internet. It is really helpful to study characteristics of the breed, such as the way the ears stand up or flap over. Study the nose—is it short or long, flat or pointed, totally visible or covered by fur? Animals' ears change when they are afraid, listening, or content. You may want to make changes to your painting to reflect a certain mood based on your studies.

Study the animal's fur to determine the length of your strokes and the direction in which to apply them.

Over and over again I hear people tell me they could never paint an animal because they don't know how to draw. But there are a couple of ways to prepare the design for the surface without feeling you need to be an expert at drawing.

1. Use a pencil and ruler to divide your photo into sections, fourths or thirds, horizontally and vertically. Prepare white paper the same size as the design in the photo. Using a ruler, draw the horizontal and vertical lines. Section by section, draw what you see in the photo. At times, turn both the photo and paper on the side or upside-down to see if the angles and lines look as accurate as possible. When you've finished drawing each section enlarge the composite drawing on a copier to the desired image size.

2. Place a piece of clear acetate over your photo and trace the major shapes, then enlarge this to the size of your surface.

Most of my work is done on canvas but I also enjoy painting on wood items. The canvas is ready to paint but the wood requires some preparation. Whether canvas or wood, I generally start my painting by applying a light gray or light blue (cool) background to the surface. I then decide upon any background elements I'd like to include, or I may want to design a surrounding area to complement the animal.

Mix your paints to match the animal's hair/fur. Whether you work in acrylics or oils, mix enough for the complete painting. Usually I like to paint the features first. (Then the animal's eyes can "watch me" complete the whole painting!) Next, consider the hair/fur. Is it short or long? You need to stroke the hair/fur as you see it. Use the chisel edge of a flat or rake brush to paint the fur, and stroke the short or long strokes unevenly. Like the hair on our heads, fur falls in layers but is not in even rows. Refer to the color worksheet on page 116 for samples of how to stroke the fur. A repeated phrase of mine is, "stroke in the direction the hair/fur lies." This is not the same for every animal. For instance, on the fore-

head of a cow, the hair has a star-like effect.

Work to have more than one value in each area. Light, medium, and dark values will give dimension. Human hair would look flat if painted with just one value. Stroke in the first color, not covering the area completely, but leaving little surface for the next color. Then stroke in a second color within the first color. Do not go back over the two colors. If you see a little area which needs to be stroked again, just make a zigzag stroke in the area. Otherwise, you will lose the different values. If the area looks rough, sometimes I will lightly comb over it with the chisel edge of a flat brush.

Rather than stroking one layer at a time, select portions of an area, then stroke the first layers of color in that area, then the second color, then gently comb if needed. Keep the strokes the same length, for instance, if the hair is short, then paint all layers with short strokes. Otherwise the short hair will turn into long hair. Work from the outside area inward toward center. The color worksheet on page 117 shows the hair direction for the kitten's head and shoulder area on the "Kitten Basket" project.

At times I'll tell my students "You can be a little shaky." Personally, I like what is sometimes referred to as the "heart-monitor stroke" (up and down uneven strokes). It gives a realistic look. A little practice will make it a natural stroke for you.

When working in acrylics, after I've completed placing all my colors I will dampen the area with the blending gel plus a little paint. Then I reapply the strokes and mixes, and soften throughout the area, working small sections, not large areas. This gives an attractive finishing touch to the painting.

When your painting is complete allow it to dry thoroughly, then apply two coats of water-based varnish to protect it.

TERMS

- *means to stroke in the first color listed, then add the second color within the first color.*

+ *means to brush-mix the colors listed and apply.*

p/ *means to add only a pindot of the paint listed.*

KITTEN BASKET PATTERN AND COLOR MAP FOR FUR

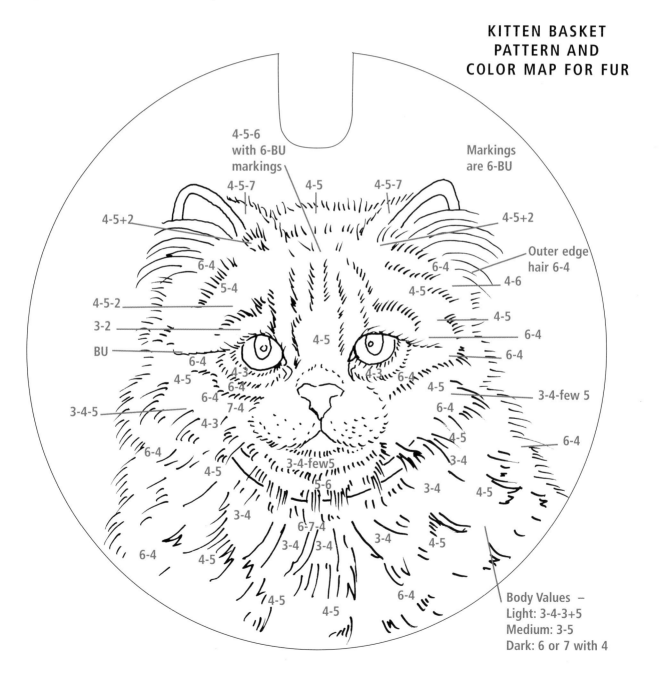

Kitten Basket

Designed by Vi Thurmond, MDA

MATERIALS

PALETTE

FolkArt Artists' Pigments:
Burnt Sienna (BS)
Burnt Umber (BU)
Cobalt Blue (CB)
Ice Blue (IB)
Pure Black (B)
Raw Sienna (RS)
Titanium White (W)
Turner's Yellow (TY)
Yellow Ochre (YO)

BRUSHES

Loew-Cornell, Inc.:
1/8" rake: *Series 7520*
#0, #1, #2, #4, #6 flat shader:
   Series 7300
Larger flat for background
10/0 liner

SURFACE

Basket with wood lid, 6¼" diameter,
   x 4¼" high from *Provo Craft*

OTHER SUPPLIES

See Basic Supplies, page 2
FolkArt Blending Gel
Transparent tape
DecoArt Oak Gel Stain
DecoArt Clear Gel
Water-based varnish

SOURCES

See page 127

INSTRUCTIONS

PREPARATION

Cover the basket areas, inside and out, with plastic wrap while painting on the lid. Sand the basket top, seal with all-purpose sealer, then sand again. Wipe free of dust.

Base both sides of the lid with two coats of Mix #1 (below), sanding lightly between coats. Allow to dry. Next, dampen with blending gel, then lighten through the center of the circle (where the face of the kitten will be) using #2. You may need to lighten a second time in order for it to hold. Transfer the pattern on page 113 to the basket lid (see Transferring the Design, page 7).

PAINTING PROCEDURE

Prepare the following paint mixes (see samples on worksheet, page 117:
1. IB+CB+p/W+p/YO (background blue/green)
2. W+p/YO (cream color)
3. W+p/RS (light, light yellow)
4. W+BS+just a p/#1
5. BS+YO+RS+BU (3:1:1:1)
6. BS+RS+BU (3:1:1)
7. BS+RS+BU+p/#1

Kitten
Step 1

Refer to the pattern/color map on page 113 and worksheet on page 117 to paint individual areas. Paint one area at a time to allow values to be added into the base.

Ears. Edge: Base #5, lighten center with touches of #4.

Inside: Base #4+#5. Shade top #7.

Stroke long hairs, using liner and thinned #4-#3-#2. Allow to dry.

Eyes. Base the Iris TY; shade bottom edge with RS (1). Paint the pupil B. Thin CB on the edge of the pupil (2). Lighten the iris with thin W (3). Shade the top of the eye with a line of B, then outline and add the tear duct with B. Highlight the iris with W all around the pupil (4). Use BU to extend the black shading above and below the eye and into the tear duct (5). Highlight with a dot of W (6).

Nose. Base BS+W; shade #7. Nostril openings are B. Lighten the top with W + BS.

Division and Mouth. The division is BU; the mouth opening is BS + BU with BU shading on both extensions.

Top of head: Strokes of #4-#5 (more #4) upward. Continue with strokes of #4-#5-#6 as listed on the color placement sheet. The darkest strokes are #7-BU. Overstroke the lighter areas overstroked #3-#2. The area may be restroked in Step 2.

Cheeks and Chin: Both cheek areas are painted with #3-#2 with shading above and next to the mouth using #3+#5-#5. The whisker markings are #3 +#5. Whiskers are stroked in after the kitten is completed using thinned #2 with #7 shading under a few whiskers.

Stroke in the outer areas of the chin using #3-#5, #3-#3-#5 in light area, and #5 next to the BS-BU mouth opening.

Sides and Body: Stroke thin #5-#7 on outer edge. Work inward, lighter values are #4-#3-#3+#5 with some #2 strokes. Shadow under the collar is #5-#6.

Collar: Base with Mix #1+CB+

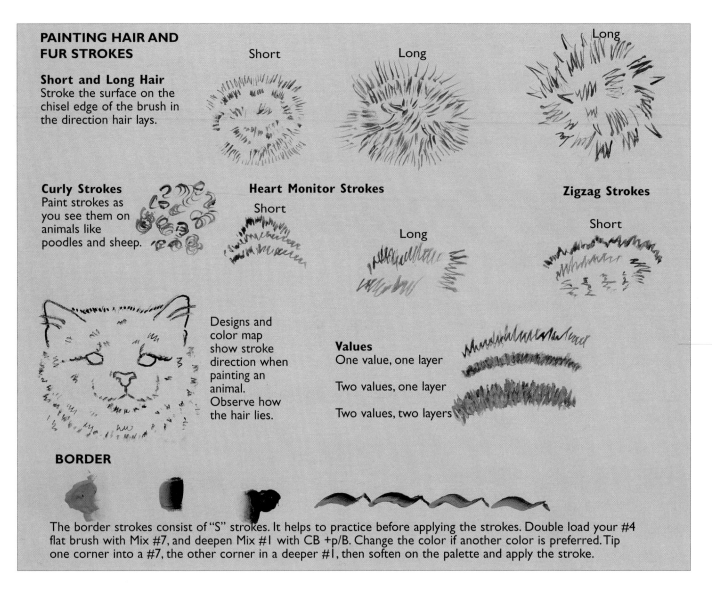

PAINTING HAIR AND FUR STROKES

Short and Long Hair
Stroke the surface on the chisel edge of the brush in the direction hair lays.

Short

Long

Long

Curly Strokes
Paint strokes as you see them on animals like poodles and sheep.

Heart Monitor Strokes

Short

Long

Zigzag Strokes

Short

Designs and color map show stroke direction when painting an animal. Observe how the hair lies.

Values
One value, one layer

Two values, one layer

Two values, two layers

BORDER

The border strokes consist of "S" strokes. It helps to practice before applying the strokes. Double load your #4 flat brush with Mix #7, and deepen Mix #1 with CB +p/B. Change the color if another color is preferred. Tip one corner into a #7, the other corner in a deeper #1, then soften on the palette and apply the stroke.

YO+W+p/B; shade with a deeper value of the base. Dry first coat.

Step 2

Dampen each area with blending gel plus a pindot of the paint mixture listed for that area. Restroke each area with the mix listed in Step 1 to refine and soften . Allow to dry thoroughly between applications.

Decorative Border

The border consists of "S" strokes (see page 35) painted around the edge of the lid to "halo" the kitty. If you haven't painted "S" strokes before, I recommend that you practice before applying the strokes to your project. Deepen Mix #1 with CB+p/B. Using your #4 flat, double load with the deepened Mix #1 and Mix #7. Change the colors if you prefer another combination. Tip one corner into #7, and the other corner into the deepened #1, then soften on the palette and apply the stroke around the edge as shown in the photo. Let dry.

FINISHING

If you want to go back into the painting to lighten or deepen, just dampen the area and make the changes you want. Allow to dry thoroughly

Cover the entire lid and leather with a circle of plastic wrap. To paint the side edge of the lid you will need to mask off both inside and out with removable tape. Paint the edge with the collar color. Mix #1+CB+YO+W+p/B. Do not remove your masking until after you've painted the basket.

Basket Finishing

Cover the entire lid and leather. Paint the band around the top of the basket and the handle with #7+BS (dark red-brown).

Stain the basket with *DecoArt Oak Gel Stain* mixed with *DecoArt Clear Gel* (more gel than stain for a light color). Try the mix on other wood first to check the depth of stain. Brush on the inside area first, then the bottom of the outside, then the sides of the basket.

Finish the lid and painted areas on the basket with two coats of a water-based varnish of your choice.

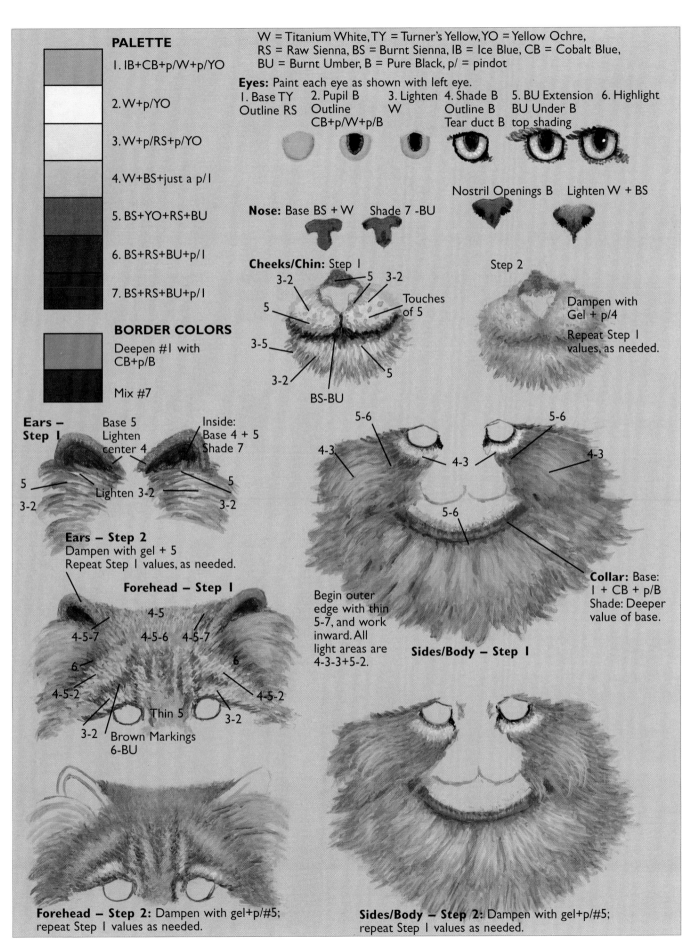

PALETTE

1. IB+CB+p/W+p/YO
2. W+p/YO
3. W+p/RS+p/YO
4. W+BS+just a p/1
5. BS+YO+RS+BU
6. BS+RS+BU+p/1
7. BS+RS+BU+p/1

BORDER COLORS

Deepen #1 with CB+p/B

Mix #7

W = Titanium White, TY = Turner's Yellow, YO = Yellow Ochre, RS = Raw Sienna, BS = Burnt Sienna, IB = Ice Blue, CB = Cobalt Blue, BU = Burnt Umber, B = Pure Black, p/ = pindot

Eyes: Paint each eye as shown with left eye.
1. Base TY Outline RS
2. Pupil B Outline CB+p/W+p/B
3. Lighten W
4. Shade B Outline B Tear duct B
5. BU Extension BU Under B top shading
6. Highlight

Nose: Base BS + W   Shade 7 -BU   Nostril Openings B   Lighten W + BS

Cheeks/Chin: Step 1   Step 2
3-2   5   3-2
5   Touches of 5
3-5
3-2   5
BS-BU

Dampen with Gel + p/4
Repeat Step 1 values, as needed.

Ears – Step 1
Base 5 Lighten center 4
Inside: Base 4 + 5 Shade 7
5   5
3-2   Lighten 3-2   3-2

Ears – Step 2
Dampen with gel + 5
Repeat Step 1 values, as needed.

Forehead – Step 1
4-5
4-5-7   4-5-6   4-5-7
6   6
4-5-2   4-5-2
3-2   Thin 5   3-2
Brown Markings 6-BU

5-6   5-6
4-3   4-3   4-3
5-6

Begin outer edge with thin 5-7, and work inward. All light areas are 4-3-3+5-2.

Sides/Body – Step 1

Collar: Base: 1 + CB + p/B Shade: Deeper value of base.

Forehead – Step 2: Dampen with gel+p/#5; repeat Step 1 values as needed.

Sides/Body – Step 2: Dampen with gel+p/#5; repeat Step 1 values as needed.

117

About Jo Sonja Jansen

Jo Sonja Jansen defines herself as a folk artist, "one who finds sheer joy in painting simple, straightforward decorations in rich and beautiful colors." She goes on to explain "many people believe a folk artist to be an untutored artist, and I could easily fit into this description." Except for fewer than two years working under a very skilled decorative artist, Jo Sonja is basically self-taught. She began sketching in childhood, then delved into oil painting in her teens and won her first art contest. The following years found her immersed in nursing school, marriage, and children, "years too busy with just plain living to devote much time to painting." Once those kids were in school, though, out came the brushes again.

This time Jo Sonja's focus was on decorative folk art. She drew inspiration from her ethnic heritage; her father was Norwegian, her mother Pennsylvania Dutch and English, with a bit of Spanish. The decorative painting style of these peoples fused into her renewed interest in painting, "an expression that refused to be denied." By 1974 Jo Sonja had earned a Master Teacher's Certificate from the Society of Decorative Painters. This same organization awarded her the Silver Palette Award in 1980 to recognize her contribution to the advancement of decorative art. Perhaps her most treasured award was the Vesterheim Gold Medal in rosemaling from the renowned Norwegian-American Museum in Decorah, Iowa, in 1996. For the last 30 years, Jo Sonja has been at the forefront of the decorative folk art revival: teaching, researching, sharing, and painting, painting, painting. She has developed a well-known line of painting supplies, but above all takes joy in participating in the international community of decorative painters. From her painting and teaching studio in the Victorian town of Eureka in far-northern California, Jo Sonja's designs have touched the world.

(top) "Victorian Ladies" relies on miniature painting techniques as well as various stroke rose styles for its inspiration.
(bottom) "Vintage Pastel Floral" is a contemporary interpretation of French and English decorative floral painting, especially the Chippendale floral techniques.
(right) Hindeloopen three-value painting was the inspiration for the softer, more blended version on the "Blue Moods" welcome board.

Folk Art Painting

By Jo Sonja Jansen, MDA, VGM

ALMOST EVERY COUNTRY HAS SOME TYPE OF FOLK ART PAINTING. WHILE usually done to decorate objects of everyday use or a special love gift, sometimes the painting became a marketable giftware item. There is recorded history of many cottage industries utilizing the painters' skills to produce items for sale. A few special items had broad enough appeal to be sold worldwide. Imagine my surprise when my husband and I discovered, in a Danish antique shop, an old German bride's box with a "saying" around the edge in Danish. Was this an imported item for resale or a special order?

Some endeavors involved more than just family members, with many different members of the village or community involved in the manufacture of painting, finishing, and shipping these objects.

Today, the interest in this type of art has sparked renewed interest in the countries of origin. We've observed many new "open-air" museums being built with the inclusion of painted wares in their displays. Also, the search for "roots" has led many to rediscover the type of folk-art painting in their heritage.

Since every folk artist was contemporary of his or her time, we should not slavishly copy the old but use our knowledge of it as a stepping stone to our own individual expression. An expression which, when joined with others of our community, will become a recognizable folk-art expression of our time.

(above) Folk-art painted cupboard from central Sweden, Province of Dalarna
(top, right) Russian Zhostova floral tray
(bottom, right) Front panel of Danish painted trunk.

Brides' Boxes

There is a rich history of painting boxes and toys in the mountain areas of Germany, Austria, Switzerland, and Northern France. Of special note are brides' boxes. Usually given to the intended bride as a love gift, these boxes would hold everything from small pins and jewelry to her special dress. The boxes came in many sizes and other items, such as small trunks, could be decorated with bits and pieces of the larger designs.

I have painted for you my own interpretation of this type of design. As an artist who loves folk art, I'm always searching for new expressions, realizing that as each folk artist was contemporary for his (or her) time, so we must be.

So... pick a color, pick a border, a figure, add maybe a bird or some houses, and then paint a love gift for someone close to you. Something special to celebrate a wedding, birthday, anniversary, or just to send "Best Wishes." The band across the bottom of the box is a perfect area to personalize the box. A date could be added in the heart.

Symbolism is often a special and meaningful part of folk art. The floral borders represent the endless succession of generations. The wavy or rickrack looking line is called the "lifeline," representing the ups and downs of life. The hearts are for love and the sprig of rosemary is for remembrance. The house represents home and a group of houses are for the village. Cross-hatching is a special protection against evil or, more specifically, protection against witches.

A bride's box folk-art design painted with traditional colors by Jo Sonja.

BRIDE'S BOX
PATTERN

Bride's Box

Designed by Jo Sonja Jansen, MDA, VGM

MATERIALS

PALETTE

Jo Sonja's Artist Colors:

Brilliant Green

Carbon Black

Napthol Crimson

Red Violet

Titanium White

Ultramarine Blue

Vermilion

Vines (background color)

Wild Grape (background color)

Yellow Deep

Optional:

Jaune Brilliant

Moss Green

Naples Yellow Hue

BRUSHES

Jo Sonja's Sure Touch Golden Taklon Brushes:

#6–#8 filbert: *Series 1385*

or ⅜" Jo Sonja's oval glaze: *Series 1390*

#3-4 round: *Series 1350*

#2 liner: *Series 1360*

#2 striping brush or long liner: *Series 1365*

1" square stroke or flat: *Series 1375*

SURFACE

Bentwood oval box, 10¾" x 7½" x 2½" from *Valhalla Designs*

OTHER SUPPLIES

See Basic Supplies, page 2

Painting medium or water

SOURCES

See page 127

INSTRUCTIONS

GENERAL INSTRUCTIONS

Note: Bentwood boxes and small trunks come from many different suppliers of woodenware and are commonly stocked by larger craft stores.

The following guidelines will be useful when selecting a brush:

- #6-8 filbert or ⅜" Jo Sonja's oval glaze: base painting of design, larger objects and sideloaded strokes for shading
- #3-4 round: base painting of design, smaller objects
- #2 liner: fine details
- #2 striping brush or long liner: painting stripes
- 1" square stroke or flat: base painting, varnishing

PREPARATION

Fill any holes in the surface with wood filler. Let dry. Sand the box well with #180-220 then fine-sand with #320-400. Wipe with a clean, damp (water) rag.

Basecoat the box with Vines (a medium value yellow-green tint). Band the box lid with Wild Grape. I painted inside the bottom of the box Wild Grape also. Wild Grape is a beautiful medium-value toned violet.

Paint inside the lid of the box with Moss Green. This is a very light value tint of yellow-green which you could easily mix from a yellow-green + white. Let the basecoat dry, sand again and recoat, if needed.

Transfer only the main lines of the patterns on pages 121 and 124. (See Transferring the Design, page 7.)

Decoration lines may be added after the base painting of the design or painted freehand.

PAINTING TECHNIQUE
Base Painting

The decoration of the box begins with the striping of the surfaces. Use very thin paint (water or medium) and colors of choice. Please see color examples for other choices.

Mix a medium value flesh color (Titanium White + Vermilion) and base faces and hands. Rinse brush.

Refer to the color worksheets on pages 125–126 and the project photo (opposite) to base paint. Use shape following strokes (note arrows on worksheet):

Violet jacket and band: Wild Grape.

Blue areas and blue flowers: Ultramarine Blue + touch of Wild Grape.

Pink areas (roses and hatband): Napthol Crimson + Titanium White + touch of Vermilion (a nice warm medium-value red).

Red-orange areas (heart and roofs): Napthol Crimson + touch Vermilion. You may like to put a touch of this color on roses (see worksheet) and for centers of blue flowers.

Yellow areas: Yellow Deep + touch of Wild Grape to tone. You may like a blush of red on one side of tulips.

White areas: Blend Titanium White + water to a transparent colorwash and stroke all areas.

Green areas: On the Wild Grape

bands, base the leaves with Vines (background color). On the green areas you can mix a blue-green (Ultramarine Blue + Brilliant Green) or olive green (Brilliant Green + touch of Napthol Crimson or Carbon Black).

When base painting is complete, dry well and erase lines.

Shading

Sideload a water-moistened brush with Ultramarine Blue or Ultramarine Blue + a touch of Wild Grape and stroke blend a hint of shadow across the forehead and down one side of face. Add simple shadows on clothing, houses, and birds. A touch of red maybe added to roses and tulips.

Shadow strokes on all objects except leaves are Red Violet + a touch of Carbon Black.

Shadow strokes on leaves are a black-green (Brilliant Green + Carbon Black). The darkness or value depends on how much contrast you like.

Face Details

Eyes: Red Violet + touch Carbon Black.

Lips: Napthol Crimson or Red Violet.

Cheeks: Very thin blush of Napthol Crimson + Vermilion (use water).

Highlights

Note: A tint is a color + white. Again how light you make a color is purely a matter of personal taste. In order to have enough

contrast, we usually make a highlight color two value steps lighter than the base color.

Highlights are white or lighter value flesh mix (more white).

Red and violet areas: Red-orange tint Napthol Crimson + Vermilion + Titanium White). Using the liner, add strokes of Jaune Brilliant to highlight roses.

Yellow areas: Yellow Deep + Titanium White or Naples Yellow Hue (optional color).

Green areas: Light value yellow-green (Yellow Deep + Brilliant Green + Titanium White) or Moss Green (optional color).

Blue areas: Lighter value blue (Ultramarine Blue + Titanium White) or a light value blue-green (Ultramarine Blue + Brilliant Green + Titanium White).

White areas: Strokes of Titanium White + water. Slowly increase amount of white so strokes are more opaque.

Dots

Pollen dots: Vermilion or Yellow Deep.

Dot border: Add white dots at outside of yellow lifeline borders on the purple band.

Patterned-dot background: Four-dot overall pattern (optional): Light blue mix.

Narrow white border line: Space pattern of double lines about ⅜" apart.

FINISH

If you have any area too light, you can tint it down with a little colorwash in the base color of the object. On white areas, colorwashes of yellow, pink, or blue, are pretty.

On the sides of the box bottom, paint vertical stripes over the Vines basecoat using your dark green mix + water.

Give the finished box 2-3 coats of a good quality varnish. I used *Jo Sonja's Water-Based Polyurethane Varnish, Satin.*

**BRIDE'S BOX LID
SIDE BORDER PATTERN**

© 2002 YoSonja ®